REBELS
FROM
WEST POINT

REBELS
FROM
WEST POINT

Gerard A. Patterson

STACKPOLE
BOOKS

First published in paperback in 2002 by
STACKPOLE BOOKS
5067 Ritter Road
Mechanicsburg, PA 17055
www.stackpolebooks.com

Cover design by Wendy A. Reynolds
Cover illustration courtesy of the Virginia Historical Society, Richmond,
  Virginia.

Printed in the United States of America

10 9 8 7 6 5 4 3 2 1

FIRST EDITION

Library of Congress Cataloging-in-Publication Data

Patterson, Gerard A.
    Rebels from West Point / Gerard A. Patterson.
        p. cm.
    Originally published: New York : Doubleday, 1987.
    Includes bibliographical references and index.
    ISBN 0-8117-2063-2
    1. Confederate States of America. Army—Officers—History.
    2. Confederate States of America. Army—Officers—Biography.
    3. United States Military Academy—Biography. 4. Generals—
    Confederate States of America—Biography. 5. United States—
    History—Civil War, 1861–1865—Biography. 6. Allegiance—
    Confederate States of America—History. I.

Title.
E545 .P38 2002
973.7'13—dc21

                                                        2002020500

To Diane, Eric and Marc

Also by the author:

DEBRIS OF BATTLE
The Wounded of Gettysburg

FROM BLUE TO GRAY
The Life of Confederate General Cadmus M. Wilcox

JUSTICE OR ATROCITY
General George E. Pickett and the Kinston, N.C. Hangings

Contents

Preface 2002

THE 2002 BICENTENNIAL of the U.S. Military Academy has provided an occasion for the printing of this new edition of *Rebels from West Point,* first published in 1987.

In the history of an institution now two centuries old, that period when war divided its graduates, faculty, and corps of cadets constitutes but a brief chapter, however cataclysmic it was.

But it is worthwhile to reflect at this time—in the context of all that has happened since—on that dramatic episode and re-examine the motivation, behavior, and contributions of those 306 graduates who went with the Confederacy.

That's because this is the group that had to anguish more than any cadet or alumnus, before or since, over those three words "duty, honor, country" that form the idealistic foundation of the academy. Yet, through the nation's tumultuous history, there have been few West Point officers, who at some point in their careers have not been confronted with some tortuous personal challenge in interpreting just what living up to that motto required of them.

No matter how difficult the dilemma facing those who followed this company of Southerners on the long gray line, there is solace in knowing that none will ever have to endure what they did. Their experience is forever woven into the lore of the academy, very much part of what one inherits at West Point today.

Acknowledgments

THIS PURSUIT OF the U.S. Military Academy graduates who went with the Confederacy has carried me over the years from West Point on the Hudson to Richmond on the James, and from Chapel Hill in North Carolina to Culp's Hill at Gettysburg, Pa.

Along the way, many kindnesses have been extended to me, and I would like to express my appreciation to, in particular, Frances Fugate, reference librarian, the Virginia Historical Society, Richmond, and her staff; Eryl Platzer, assistant director, and Dywana M. Saunders, curatorial assistant, the Valentine Museum, Richmond; Betty Anne Stroup, director of the Mt. Lebanon, Pa., Public Library and her staff, especially for assistance in obtaining rare works through interlibrary services, and Wendy Whitfield, U.S. Military Academy Archives.

I wish to thank also the staffs of the Georgia Department of Archives and History, Atlanta; Walter Royal Davis Library, University of North Carolina, Chapel Hill; Virginia State Library, Richmond; New York Public Library and New-York Historical Society, New York City; Library of Congress, Washington, D.C., and the U.S. Army's Military History Institute, Carlisle Barracks, Pa.

Help came from many quarters. Douglas R. Jones of King, N.C., a buff, generously responded to my query in the North Carolina Civil War Roundtable newsletter to authenticate an elusive reference while Robert Castle Skrabski of Bethel Park, Pa., assisted me immeasurably by painstakingly reviewing the manuscript and mending many flaws in its presentation.

I am grateful also to Ed Holm, editor of *American History Illustrated*, for publishing in April 1985 my article on the Rebels from West Point and stimulating interest in this book-length treatment of them.

Finally, I would like to thank my wife, Diane, for encouraging me to see the project through while realizing—as ambivalently as I—that when we reached this point I would probably be surrendering a cherished avocation.

G.A.P.

Foreword

THIS IS THE STORY of the small body of men that was probably most responsible for turning the American Civil War into the costliest conflict in which the nation has ever been involved.

Virtually none of these men played any active part in bringing about the war. They entered it, for the most part, with deep regret; and they participated in a way that was strangely detached from those they led.

They were the 306 graduates of the United States Military Academy at West Point who used their training and skills to organize and lead the soldiers of the Confederate Army against the flag they had previously served.[1]

The influence and the achievements of these men were enormous. Without their assistance, there is no doubt that the Confederacy could never have fielded forces of the military caliber and proficiency of the Army of Northern Virginia and the Army of Tennessee. Their contributions made it possible for the South to carry on a war for four years against an adversary who, based on numerical strength and material resources alone, could have been expected to overwhelm it in months.

It was a historically unique role that these West Pointers performed. In choosing their side, they were of necessity aligning themselves against Union officers who once had been their classmates at the academy; against men with whom they had first experienced combat at Chapultepec, Buena Vista, and the other battles in Mexico; against men with whom they had endured hard days of escort duty along the Santa Fe trail and spent many long evenings playing faro and brag in the barracks at Fort Riley, Laramie, and other remote posts on the western frontier.

So well did they know their opponents that they could anticipate each other in a way few military leaders have been able to divine their enemies' actions. And so well acquainted were they that no matter how the war intensified in fury, nor how bitter became the feelings of those they represented, few could ever engender any personal animosity for their counterparts in the Federal camps. Their association, "this entente cordiale between us old fellows," as Confederate General George E. Pickett would call it, was too carefully woven.[2]

Much like the Royal Air Force pilots in World War II, this relative handful of formally trained officers represented "the few" upon whom the Confederacy relied. Their skills were among the South's most limited resources, and as they were lost the Rebel armies steadily weakened. Nearly one fourth of these officers would be killed in action during the war, the casualty rate accelerating rapidly in the latter stages as their cause became more desperate and the need for closer, more direct leadership in battle increased. For most of the survivors, however, the surrender at Appomattox marked only the beginning of a more difficult struggle, one which found them striving for existence as pathetic misfits in the civilian world to which their defeat consigned them.

The West Pointers written about here are primarily those who served with the Army of Northern Virginia under a commander who had himself once been superintendent of the U. S. Military Academy—Robert E. Lee. They numbered about a third of all those who went with the Confederacy; but in looking at the members of that element, their personalities and manner, the problems they faced, their relations both with the nonprofessionals with whom they shared command and with one another, one can gain an appreciation of this entire company. It was a singular group of Americans who, because of circumstances over which they held little sway, had to suffer most deeply the tragic effects of the nation's disunion.

List of Illustrations

Come fill your glasses, fellows, and stand up in a row,
    To singing sentimentally, we're going far to go.
In the army there's sobriety, promotion's very slow,
    So we'll sing our reminiscences of Benny Havens, oh!
Oh! Benny Havens, oh! Oh! Benny Havens, oh! . . .

1

"It Is a Good Cause"

THERE WAS LITTLE that was glamorous or martially glorious about army service on the western frontier during the decade following the Mexican War. The image of the sturdily palisaded fort with comfortable barracks, sutler's store, officers and their ladies quick-stepping to the fiddler at the weekly dances, and troops responding to the barked commands of sergeants on spacious parade grounds, was an illusion cruelly dispelled in an instant when a transferred soldier arrived at one of these sorry "bastions" after making his way across half a continent.

In most cases, quarters for officers and enlisted men at the seventy-nine forts spread throughout the territories were only such as the soldiers could construct themselves of the materials and tools at hand.[1] Witness one young lieutenant's introduction when, after a month's journey, he reached what was indicated on the maps and his orders as Fort Inge on the tepid Leona River in New Mexico and found himself standing in front of a crude structure built of rough poles, unmatched in length or shape, with its many open chinks daubed with mud. The roof was thatched and the floors formed of creaking, uneven boards sawed by hand. To the shavetail, "all was as unsightly as it was comfortless."

The nearest settlement, he discovered to his further chagrin, was San Antonio, ninety-eight miles to the east, and his only knowledge of that community would be as a place from "whence our mail came by courier once a week."

Aware, certainly, of how shocked she would be by the living conditions at this desolate post, but compelled by loneliness, the officer sent for his wife to join him and she dutifully complied. However, "it was some years before she ever met any of the wives of other officers of the regiment," so widely spaced were the forts.[2]

One outpost did not differ a great deal from another. Even so dedicated and austere a soldier as Lieutenant Colonel Lee, serving with the 2nd Cavalry at Fort Mason in western Texas, far from the gracious life of Arlington, could not conceal his misery when he wrote to his kin: "I wish there was anything interesting here to relate to you but we are in a desert of dullness out of which nothing is drawn."[3]

Encounters with "hostiles" were few and usually frustrating. Most often they involved a dogged, dusty pursuit after a raiding party dragging on over hundreds of miles, and a slow trek back to the fort without ever getting a glimpse of the fleeing enemy, whether Apache or Cheyenne.

Such hard, dreary service was bound to change men, even the strictly developed regular army officers from West Point. Cut off from civilization and refined society, their habits loosened. Speech became crude, dress grew careless, relationships with superiors and subordinates more casual. Self-control also slackened and men who never drank before turned to the bottle to lift their spirits or gambled far more than they could afford, not for the money that might be won but merely to idle away the hours. With every officer virtually frozen in rank in a peacetime army that numbered only 16,000 men, ambition was probably the greatest hardship to endure during that period.

To add to their few comforts and no doubt enliven their existence, many of the frontier officers engaged in private commercial ventures. One officer at San Antonio became a partner in a cattle ranch;[4] two $60-a-month lieutenants in California drew on their boyhood farming experiences to put in a crop of wheat.[5] Sometimes they became professional hunters, stocking first their own mess and then sending their orderlies to market with what game was left from their expeditions.

Very slowly did these roughened, all-but-forgotten men, far removed from the uproar and excitement in what they called "the States," become aware of the seriousness of what was stirring back there over slavery and other issues as the decade of the 1860s began.

John Brown and Harpers Ferry. The admission of Kansas and Nebraska. The Lincoln-Douglas debates. All were subjects that intimately concerned these officers, particularly those from the South. If ever the sectional turmoil should lead to civil war they knew too well that they would have to make a choice between continuing to serve the U.S. Government or returning to the states in which they were born and raised. Yet few persons were more out of touch than they, few so sketchily and belatedly informed of what was transpiring. As the rift grew, the hunger for news among the regular army soldiers became nearly unbearable. At one fort on the table-flat New Mexico plain, men would climb to the roofs of the adobe buildings and stand in clusters for hours scanning the desert for the dust of an expected mail wagon bearing news from the East.

It was a long time between mail calls at this post, too. "Our mails were due semi-monthly, but during winter seasons we were glad to have them once a month, and occasionally had to be content with once in six weeks," explained one officer to give an idea of the terms of suspense and anxiety they had to endure.[6]

During the tense period of uncertainty there was one instance in which a Union-leaning officer named Phil Sheridan flatly refused to obey an official order to transfer his command in California to a captain from Maryland named

James Archer, because he had been notified that Archer intended "to go South" and feared "some rebellious act."[7]

Sheridan was not just being an alarmist. Two Southern officers actually had conspired to surrender the entire U.S. 2nd Cavalry regiment in Texas to Secession authorities. Finally, the pair had permitted the unit to sail for New York but only after stripping it of its arms, ruining its morale, and attempting unsuccessfully to recruit the troopers for Confederate service.[8]

Among most men in the army there was until the last a fervent hope that the breach would somehow be sealed without their being forced to take sides against one another. At West Point, the counsel of the Southern-born superintendent to a restless cadet from Louisiana was, "Watch me; when I jump, you jump. What's the use of jumping too soon?"[9]

After South Carolina formally withdrew from the Union, a few officers wrote letters to the adjutant general resigning their commissions. More such letters were submitted after the formation of the Confederacy by the seceding states, but the bulk of the Southern officers waited until after the attack on Fort Sumter, and after Lincoln's call for troops, to quit the service and start home.

In doing this, the West Pointers were plainly aware of what they were forfeiting in terms of pensions, allowances, and career investment. What they could not evaluate was the legal risk they were taking. If they were to be captured or the Confederate effort to fail, would their action be construed as desertion to take up arms for the enemy, a crime for which the usual penalty was execution? Who could say? Such a situation had never been faced.

Lieutenant Dorsey Pender of the First Dragoons wrote his young wife in North Carolina of his decision and tried to ease her concern: "My own dear wife, don't trouble yourself. Recollect that those who do not go into this are the exceptions. It is a good cause."[10]

With remarkable analytical acumen for a man so young, Lieutenant James B. McPherson of Ohio, stationed on dreary

Alcatraz Island in San Francisco Bay, wrote a prophetic letter to his friend, Lieutenant E. P. Alexander of Georgia, a few days after the latter had resigned:

"This war is not going to be the ninety days affair that papers and politicians are predicting. Both sides are in deadly earnest, and it is going to be fought out to the bitter end. . . . For your cause, there can be but one result. It must be lost. Your whole population is about eight millions, three millions are slaves who may become an element of danger. You have no army, no navy, no treasury, and practically none of the manufactures and machine shops necessary for the support of armies, and for war on a large scale. You are but scattered agricultural communities, and you will be cut off from the rest of the world by blockade. Your cause is fore-doomed to failure."[11]

In the mess hall at the military academy, when word of the fall of Fort Sumter was read to the assembled corps, the cadets stood and sang "The Star-Spangled Banner." One remembered, "It was the first time I ever saw the Southern contingent cowed."[12] The next day, many of the boys from Dixie left the post and followed the majestic Hudson River up to Albany to return home by rail. Ordinarily they would have travelled by way of New York, but feelings were running so high they feared mob action were they to be recognized in that city. When Lieutenant Fitzhugh Lee, an instructor of cavalry tactics who was extremely popular with the cadets, decided to return to Virginia he was serenaded by a group of plebes who were saddened to see him go but appreciated the position in which he had been placed.[13]

Unknowingly revealing how desperately torn he was in his sense of responsibility, before departing to join the Confederates Captain Dabney Maury of Virginia sat down with the U.S. Army officer succeeding him in command of a fort in Texas and, as if he were simply being transferred to some other post, carefully explained to him how he had distributed the troops of the department.[14]

While he remained at his post in the Department of

Utah as commander of the Second Dragoons, a colonel from Virginia named Philip St. George Cooke had to suffer the anguish of having his son, Lieutenant John R. Cooke of the 8th U.S. Infantry, leave the service to go South as well as his son-in-law, a twenty-eight-year-old 1st Cavalry captain named James E. B. Stuart. The colonel could not bring himself to turn against the old flag. His first allegiance was to the Union, not to Virginia. Of their painful situation, Captain Stuart wrote his brother-in-law, "It is a sad thing but the responsibility of the present state of our separation in the family rests entirely with the Colonel. Let us bear our misfortune in silence."[15]

At an adobe post in California, when the breakup came an officer from Pennsylvania named Winfield Scott Hancock arranged a farewell party for a group of his fellow officers who were returning South together. It was a time to be sentimental and the young men clustered about Mrs. Hancock's piano and sang familiar army ballads that must have sounded strange to the Mexican families that surrounded the quarters. When the inevitable moment came to part, and hilarity could no longer mask their deep sadness, an old friend of Hancock, Captain Lewis Armistead, a crusty widower who had buried his wife out on the frontier, clasped his hand and said feelingly, "You can never know what this has cost me."[16]

Though hardly an emotional man, Major James Longstreet, paymaster at the army post at Albuquerque, also felt profoundly his withdrawal from the regular army.

"It was a sad day when we took leave of lifetime comrades and gave up a service of twenty years," he wrote. "Neither Union officers nor their families made efforts to conceal feelings of deepest regret. When we drove out from the post, a number of officers rode with us, which only made the last farewell more trying."[17]

After crossing the Rio Grande en route to the Confederacy, Longstreet had a curious encounter with a sergeant of the Mounted Rifle Regiment who stated that he was from

Virginia and would like to join the officer and return to his native state with several other enlisted men who would serve as Longstreet's escort.

Demonstrating how he, for one, interpreted his legal position in leaving the U.S. Army, Longstreet admonished the sergeant to return to his post and "explained that private soldiers could not go without authority from the War Department; that it was different with commissioned officers, in that the latter could resign their commissions, and when the resignations were accepted they were independent of military authority, and could, as other citizens, take such action as they might choose, but that he and his comrades had enlisted for a specified term of years, and by their oaths were bound to the term of enlistment."[18]

For those on duty at the most distant forts on the Pacific Coast, it would take months to reach home. Such was the fervor of the Southern population, however, that these late arrivals found themselves being snubbed as hesitant, lukewarm secessionists. Captain George E. Pickett, stationed in the Washington Territory when the war erupted, had sailed from San Francisco around South America to New York and then made his way to Canada, finally reaching Virginia via Kentucky in September of 1861, months after the first battle at Manassas had been fought. Yet on arriving in Richmond after his awesome journey, Pickett found "so bitter is the feeling here that my being unavoidably delayed so long in avowing my allegiance to my state has been most cruelly and severely criticized by friends, yes, and even relatives."[19]

Lafayette McLaws, a 6th Infantry captain, had to make his way back from New Mexico and gave this description of his trek:

"The snow being too deep to cross the plains from Santa Fe, myself and two other officers worked our way to El Paso, Mexico, to take passage in the overland mail stages, along the route of the 32nd parallel but finding that the Apaches had driven the stage from route coming from California side and the Comanches had possession of the route from El Paso to the States east, we worked our way in a wagon to Fort Davis and then hiring a stage traveled day and night until we reached Jeffersonville, Mo., and then went to St. Louis where we first received authentic statements in regard to the secession of the Southern states, my native state, Georgia, being among the number."[20]

No one went to such lengths to make his way South as Gustavus Smith, an 1842 graduate who had long ago resigned his commission in the Corps of Engineers to become street commissioner of the City of New York. To get away from that city unnoticed, the very public official first feigned serious illness and then "ostensibly died and a handsome coffin containing bricks was buried with honors" while Smith, in disguise, slipped out of town.[21]

Needless to say, the Federal authorities were furious over the number of officers, trained at the taxpayers' expense, who were "going South."

"The large disaffection at the present crisis of United States Army officers has excited the most profound astonishment and naturally provokes inquiry as to its cause," Secretary of War Simon Cameron stated in a report on July 1, 1861. "But for this startling defection the rebellion never could have assumed formidable proportions. . . . The majority of these officers solicited and obtained a military education at the hands of the government—a mark of special favor confined by the laws of Congress to only one in 70,000 inhabitants.

"At the national Military Academy they were received and treated as the adopted children of the republic. By the peculiar relations thus established they virtually became bound by more than ordinary obligations of honor to remain faithful to their flag. The question may be asked in view of this extraordinary treachery displayed whether its promoting cause may not be traced to a radical defect in the system of education itself."[22]

Lincoln himself showed his anger in a message to Congress on July 4 of that year when he alluded to the "large

numbers of those in the army and navy who have been favored as officers [who] have resigned and proved false to the
land which had pampered them."[23]

As they came into the Confederacy, the long-absent officers (after perhaps spending a brief time becoming reac-
quainted with families and neighbors who had all but forgotten their faces) began offering their services to the governors
or the ranking militia officers at their state capitals, and were
given their commissions and assignments. They by no means
got off to an even and equal start. An army captain of eight
years' experience might, in Alabama, land a colonel's stars
and wreath and the command of a regiment, whereas in
Georgia he might obtain only a major's rank and command of
a battery. In most instances, an officer's initial rank depended
on what his state's policy was toward grading regular army
officers who joined its forces. In many cases, that depended
on connections. It was a turbulent period and actions were
being taken hastily. Often a strong endorsement from a powerful state figure who might be a family friend was enough to
win even a lieutenant a field grade appointment. When the
units were drawn into the regular Confederate states army,
the West Pointers usually were quickly elevated to positions
of more authority and their ranks adjusted; but by no means
was there ever a strict ratio observed between an officer's
standing in the old army and his station in the new one.

Only a little more than half of the academy-trained officers coming into the Confederacy had actually been on
active duty with the army. The others had abandoned their
army careers for various and sundry reasons—lack of advancement, the boredom of peacetime garrison duty, a loss
of taste for the military life. Those who had left the service
had ventured in numerous directions. Many had put their
engineering training to use in the lucrative and far more
stimulating railroad industry. Jubal Early, class of '37, came
back to the army from Franklin County, Virginia, where he
had been a lawyer and prosecutor since leaving the service

less than two years after his graduation. Daniel Harvey Hill, class of '42, left the supervision of the North Carolina Military Institute to join the Southern forces. His brother-in-law who had done such good service in Mexico but who had long since been forgotten—Thomas J. Jackson—gave up his dual post of professor of natural philosophy and instructor of artillery tactics at the Virginia Military Institute. William N. Pendleton, class of '30, now the Reverend Pendleton, came down from the pulpit of Grace Episcopal Church in Lexington, Virginia, to enter the fray.

In their strange new tunics of gray with gold facing and gorgeous knots of braid woven on the sleeves, the younger ones with French *kepis* tilted jauntily on their heads, the West Pointers—their breach complete—rode out to the teeming Rebel camps to take up their work. The decision had been made; there was no point in dwelling on it anymore. In fact, they suddenly realized there would be little time to reflect on anything after getting but a glimpse of the task that awaited them. It made little difference whether their initial exposure to their charges was gained at the state capitals to which they had flocked, or at the central locations in Virginia and Tennessee where the major armies were being assembled. All the sites presented similar scenes of chaos.

Disorganized mobs of volunteers awaited their attention in sprawling camps of tents and makeshift huts set up haphazardly on every patch of green. It seemed that no one had given a thought to the placing of sentries, or to security of any kind. For all their imposing finery, the arriving officers earned few military salutes and tried not to appear too shocked when they received a wave instead.

The most formidable aspect of the groups were the names they had given themselves—the Amherst Rough and Readys, the Allegheny Rifles, the Appomattox Greys, the Brunswick Guard, the Louisiana Tigers.

Clothing ranged from the coarse homespun of the mountain men to the dashing, red-pantalooned *Zouave* attire of some of the New Orleans companies and the orange-and-blue elegance of the historic Maryland Line. The maidens of Richmond sighed over the splendor of the 1st South Carolina Regiment boys in their silver-trimmed gray uniforms as they strode down Main Street to their camps. They would swoon again at the sight of the young men of the 1st Virginia Cavalry in their plumed hats and brass-buttoned tunics, every rider magnificently mounted. But most of the troops came in wearing plain home-tailored outfits of whatever shade of gray cloth could be had locally and the same felt hats they wore every day in the fields.

While many of the volunteers were unarmed, the men who would tutor them observed that some were equipped with so many weapons it was doubtful they could transport, never mind use, all of them. Rifles bristled with bayonets, and belts were stuffed with bowie knives, Colts, and derringers.

Company officers, selected on the basis of their geniality, exercised little control over the troops, mixing with the men so familiarly that they could rarely be distinguished from them.

Lieutenant Colonel (and until very recently U.S. Army Captain) Henry "Harry" Heth was something of a legend at West Point for his outrageous pranks, and he needed all his sense of humor in his new endeavor. Describing what it was like in those early days of formation, he recalled:

"As companies reported for duty I mustered them into the service, taught them, or tried to teach them, how to make out their muster rolls, issued to them tents, knapsacks, etc. Night schools for the officers were organized and tactics given them to study. But I found that some could not read, so schools were abandoned. When ten companies reported, a regiment was formed and it received its number from Richmond. While this was going on, the commissary, quartermaster, ordnance and medical experts departments had to be organized. It will be readily seen that I had no time to play. I had no one to assist me."[24]

Discipline and control were not achieved without resistance, as might be expected. A soldier of the 11th Georgia, quartered on the fair grounds at Richmond since arriving by rail, said of his unit's first months in service under the domination of regular army officers:

"There has perhaps been no time since our enlistment during which the members of this regiment manifested such a general spirit of dissatisfaction, such restlessness under restraint, such murmurings at authority and such complaints against the intolerable hardships of the war. We had enlisted to fight Yankees, not to sweep yards, clean away trash, stand guard in the rain and, in short, embark in a general system of doing drudgery. And then to be compelled to ask a white man, no whiter than ourselves, for a pass in order to go beyond the guard lines, was such a discount upon the gentlemanly estimates we had formed of our gentlemanly selves."[25]

Some help was being provided in drilling troops by shrill-voiced, nattily-dressed cadets from the Virginia Military Institute and other schools, and here and there conscientious volunteer officers were developing themselves with the aid of textbooks and imparting their freshly acquired knowledge to their men. But for all intents and purposes, it would be up to the West Pointers to fashion the eager horde into an army.

As they tackled the tasks of organization, supply, and drill, they were not surprised to see that the military force they were creating was, at least on paper, almost exactly the same as the regular U.S. Army. The regulations they adopted were those that they themselves had lived by in that army; staffs were structured much as they were there; marching formations and practices, battle arrangements, and artillery drills were the very ones being practiced in the Union camps. But there the similarity between the two armies ended, for the material was different.

Probably the biggest adjustment the regulars had to make in their new roles was learning to adapt themselves to the manner and nature of the Confederate enlistees in the ranks. Directing these predominantly unschooled, rustic, unpretentious, sunny-natured, highly informal and stubbornly independent young men was proving to be a trying, exasperating, and sometimes highly amusing experience. Only the officers who could master the technique seemed to hold any hope for success in the new army.

Not untypical was the experience of a general officer who went up to a sentry he found comfortably seated at a post and asked, "What are you doing here, my man?"

"Nothin' much, jes' kinder takin' care of this hyar stuff," was the reply the guard delivered, not thinking to stand up, never mind salute.

"Do you know who I am, sir?"

"Well, now 'pears like I know your face, but I can't jes' call your name—who is you?"

"I'm General Wigfall."

"General, I'm pleased to meet you—my name's Jones," the private said, extending his hand in friendship but still not bothering to rise to his feet.[26]

Few of the leaders were regarded with any degree of awe by the privates who, from the beginning, did not hesitate to voice their sentiments freely to their superiors. In one instance a well-mounted, handsomely dressed officer began shouting down to some Texas infantrymen sloshing their way along a road that had become a quagmire, "Hurry up, men, hurry up, don't mind a little mud."

A private looked up at him and brazenly asked, "D'ye call this a little mud? Suppose ye get down and try it, stranger. I'll hold your horse."

"Do you know whom you address, sir?" the aghast officer called out. "I'm General Whiting!"

"General!" the Texan shot right back. "Don't you reckon I know a general from a long-tongued courier?"[27]

When the officers took their regiments to the places where the units were being assembled into armies—the vicinity of Centreville for the one being formed in Virginia—

they found confusion on a grander scale and the labors and frustrations exhausting. But at night the West Pointers did have the pleasure of looking up old friends and trading gripes about the shortages of provisions and the obstinacies of their recruits, as well as exchanging any information they might have on the status and whereabouts of other classmates or friends.

As in all society, age was somewhat a divider and the officers tended to mingle with men from academy classes of the same period as their own. Those older than thirty-five had for the most part been in Mexico together, some following Zachary Taylor on his "glory march" to the City of Mexico, others having missed those great opportunities at Monterey, Buena Vista, and Palo Alto while serving with Winfield Scott in the less active wing of the army.

The officers under thirty-five would have been too young for the Mexican War but the senior of this group could date his service from the fights with the Comanches in Texas and the Apaches in the Southwest. Any man over twenty-five might have taken part in what the military called simply "the Utah expedition," the 1857 march from Fort Leavenworth to put an end to alleged acts of defiance against the government by members of the Mormon sect.

A good percentage of all of the regular army officers had at one time or another pulled a tour as instructor at the military academy or, in the case of cavalrymen and dragoons, at the cavalry school at Carlisle Barracks in Pennsylvania, not far from Gettysburg. A fortunate few might be able to count among the highlights of their careers to date an observer's mission abroad.

The men who had been assigned to the military academy during that period between the wars would often reflect on it as one of the most pleasant periods of their service. A Napoleon Club and a Spanish Club both were eagerly supported by the officers who had served in Mexico, learning something of the language from the señoritas and adding some practical lessons in warfare to what they had received on the blackboards at West Point. Naturally, it was an ever-changing faculty group and a relaxed, unaffected one mainly because all its members, said one officer, had had a chance to "wash off the starch of the academy in a few years of active service." Such was the atmosphere that the arrival of an old comrade or of a foreign officer was all that was needed "to start the champagne corks popping."[28]

At any rate, these experiences they had shared to one degree or another, depending on their length of service, were recalled and exaggerated as they met now as Confederates in new and strange garb and in a setting to which they were still trying to accustom themselves. When they did get together there was generally a good deal of drinking and, inevitably, card playing. Riding competitions were also popular among these men who considered horsemanship one of the most essential social graces. Sometimes these gatherings of old chums managed to get out of hand, and rumors spread through the camps like lice of the wild scenes of debauchery at one tent or another.[29]

The men in the ranks, so unfamiliar with military types yet swept up with warlike ardor, found the veteran officers to be a fascinating group and observed them closely, giving each a nickname based on some prominent mannerism or physical characteristic. Nervous, fussy Cadmus Marcellus Wilcox of Tennessee readily became "Old Billy Fixing." The clear-domed dragoon, Richard S. Ewell, was "Old Baldy," and predictably, Jubal Early was soon "Old Jubilee." Lafayette McLaws, a stickler for regulations, was "General Make Laws" to his men.

The headquarters guard could not help but notice that the younger officers from the regular army that he saw, those more recently out of the academy, seemed somewhat neater, more formal and correct than the older ones. The longer the men had been out in the territories, the saltier they appeared. The profanity of some, the sentries and escorts found, was enough to turn the air blue, particularly the language spoken in a comical lisp by the doughty Ewell. A high-bred cavalryman recalled Ewell as the "most violently and elaborately profane man I ever knew" because his profanity did not consist of a single or even a double oath but was ingeniously wrought into whole sentences.[30]

For their part, the West Pointers appeared to enjoy some of the looser aspects of this new army and the release from the discipline of the regular army. This was evidenced particularly in the way they began to dress. As a rule, the officers who did possess a regulation Confederate uniform kept it carefully folded in a camp trunk for donning only on social forays. What they wore in camp and on the march could most charitably be described as picturesque.

The just-mentioned Cadmus Wilcox could dress like a baron when he was to pose for a daguerreotype at a Richmond studio but about his headquarters he was much more readily recognized in a short, round jacket and a broad-brimmed straw hat; when mounted on the old white pony he favored, he could be seen using a long hickory switch for a crop. "Jube" Early liked to wear a large white felt hat, ornamented by a dark ostrich feather and an immense white, full cloth overcoat that extended all the way to his heels.

In adapting themselves to the relative informality of this new army, some of the regulars made the mistake on occasion of letting themselves be carried too far by the tide of democracy. For example, General Arnold Elzey, a former 2nd Artillery captain, was known to be quite fond of a dram. One night when he and his staff were drinking quite freely, and feeling quite liberal, Elzey called in the sentry who was on guard at his quarters and gave him a taste before retiring for the night. About daylight, when this same sentinel was on post again, he poked his head in the tent door and finding the general still asleep, woke him up by exclaiming, "General! General! Ain't it about time for us to take another drink?"

Elzey roused himself and, not being in as merry a mood as the night before, ordered the man taken off to the guardhouse for his insolence.[31]

Some of the West Pointers would never bend and insisted from the beginning on treating the rustic volunteers under them as U.S. Army regulars. Johnny Reb could not tolerate this stuffy, aloof type of officer. General George Pickett of Virginia, for instance, got off to a bad start with his first command by showing himself as a "spit-and-polish" type leader. At his very first inspection of the 8th Virginia Regiment, he paused in front of one private and took up his gun. When he rubbed his white glove over the barrel and came away with a rust streak, he stared at it as if he were about to retch. When the colonel at his side intervened on behalf of the private to say, "General, this young man left college in the North to come South and fight with us," Pickett's only response was to whip out a handkerchief, give it a nasal blast, and move on.[32]

More deeply humiliating to the enlisted men were the genuinely cruel disciplinarians among the West Pointers, men of General George "Maryland" Steuart's stamp. A 1st Cavalry captain and longtime Indian fighter, Steuart was a tough and nasty martinet and soon showed his power to the militarily ignorant Confederates in his command. It was not uncommon in his camp to see two or three men tied up by the thumbs to a cross pole.

One night he got his deserts when practicing his favorite ruse of sneaking up on sentries and trying to catch them unawares. A private he thus startled grabbed hold of the little leader and pummeled him mercilessly, afterwards pretending not to have recognized the general.[33]

The vast majority of the West Pointers who had come South soon realized that rigid discipline was not the way to move the kind of young men they had in their ranks. The officers developing the most responsive and spirited commands were those who were quickest to abandon their "old army" ways and accept the informal, footloose Confederate for what he was, making no attempt to mold him into a Coldstream Guard. He simply would not permit it.

2

"The Entente Cordiale"

THE SOUTHERN VOLUNTEERS who felt put upon by the "West P'inters" when ordered to dig latrines about the campgrounds for sanitation or to remain on their feet while on sentry duty quickly learned there were more severe dimensions to soldiering, when the regulars took them into the field in the spring of 1862 and the war began in earnest.

On the march, the struggling, panting men in the ranks found out they were expected to keep up no matter what distances were set even if their feet blistered or their canteens ran dry. If they lagged behind in the presence of some of their leaders, they were liable to feel the flat of a sword against their backs to spur them forward. The harshest realization of what they were signed up for came to the troops assigned to that peculiar professor from the Virginia Military Institute, Thomas J. Jackson, when they were marched more than 250 miles up and down the Shenandoah Valley in the course of a one-month campaign. Often they retraced roads from which their own footprints had not yet disappeared as their odd leader sought to compensate with mobility for the disparity of numbers between his men and three separate Federal forces. When the taciturn leader, unrecognizable as a general in his shabby garb, overheard one exhausted man complain of the way they were being driven he graced him with a brief explanation. "It's for your own good, sir," he said.[1]

Predictably, the excess gear with which the men started the campaign was soon littering the roadsides and marking their passing: overcoats, bayonets, books, derringers, and battered shoes. It was not long before the infantrymen were stripped down to the essentials for field duty: Enfield or Springfield rifles and ramrods, brimmed felt hats, blanket rolls slung over the shoulder, haversacks, canteens, cartridges stuffed in pockets, shirts, jackets and trousers of whatever description, shoes if serviceable. Thus unencumbered, they would in time amaze themselves as well as their foes with the distances they could cover. Men of A. P. Hill's Light Division once marched seventeen miles in seven hours as a cohesive unit from Harpers Ferry to Sharpsburg; an Alabama brigade covered the eighteen miles from New Guilford to Gettysburg in even less time when needed.

How an officer handled his troops on the march became one gauge of his effectiveness. When one Virginia brigadier was killed, a sergeant lamented that "he always made the men take care of themselves as best they could" and reflected on how in his unit, when about to ford a stream, every man was required to remove his shoes because the officer knew from long experience how the leather of wet shoes would tear up a soldier's feet when it dried and hardened.[2]

When it came time for the battlefield, the main instructional task of the West Pointers—aside from helping to overcome fright—was convincing these independent-minded rustic youths of the importance of concentrating their firepower. Success would come to the side that could mass its weapons and move in close to use them. This meant holding formation, guiding on their battle flags, discharging their rifles only when ordered; and not leaving ranks under any excuse, whether to aid an injured comrade, look for water, or give way to fear. Gradually, as they were exposed to combat, the men themselves began to see even through the din and confusion what their leaders were emphasizing. To do damage, their work with the rifle had to be concerted. They grew to respect those units that closed with the enemy, and to deride regiments with reputations for firing at long range, making a great deal of noise but inflicting or sustaining few casualties. Not that they would ever master any textbook maneuvers on the field. As one Southern general would put it later, "Who ever saw a Confederate line advance that was not as crooked as a ram's horn?"[3]

The raw recruits' first exposure to combat was a crucial time for their instructors, as well, and most of the latter sensed how closely they were being scrutinized by their understandably frightened troops. It was up to them, the veterans, to demonstrate that it was something that could be borne.

A private in a Texas regiment, going into action for the first time at Gaines Mill, admitted "I got mighty nervous and shaky." But when he looked behind him and saw John Bell Hood, a towering blond commander who had been an Indian fighter of some reknown with the U. S. 2nd Cavalry, resting on one foot, his arm raised above his head, his hand grasping the limb of a tree, looking as unconcerned as if he were on dress parade, the private determined that "if he could stand it, I would."[4]

The West Pointers had to demonstrate their toughness to the untrained officers under them as well as to the men in the ranks. A Virginia lawyer-turned-soldier would never forget the response he got when he appealed to his brigadier, the gruff Nathan "Shanks" Evans, for reinforcements at the battle of Ball's Bluff:

"Tell Hunton to hold the ground until every damn man falls."[5]

"Does anyone really know Lee?" a Richmond matron inquired of her guests as they discussed with some anxiety his selection by President Davis to succeed the wounded General Joseph E. Johnston early in the war at a time when the Federals under General George B. McClellan were threatening the Southern capital. "He looks so cold, quiet and grand."[6]

There was something awesome indeed about the graying, superbly poised leader who had unexpectedly arrived on the scene. The enlisted men in the camps who turned from their fires, card games, or chores to study the graceful horseman trot by on his initial inspection of his command, trailed by a staff of impeccably uniformed young gentlemen, noted his calmness and seeming imperturbability, his ruddy, robust complexion, and the unusually muscular, thick-necked form of the man who was then in his fifty-fifth year. He had been seen about occasionally before his appointment during the period when he was serving as the president's military advisor, but few knew who he was. Some of the volunteers now recalled seeing the name "R. E. Lee" in newspaper accounts of his abortive West Virginia campaign during the first months of the war.

Unfamiliar as he was to the private in the ranks, Lee was as well known to the officer corps as any other West Point man who had "gone South" with the regulars.

Lee's prewar career had been long and varied and he had come into personal contact at some time or post with a large percentage of the professional soldiers now with the army. Some were cadets at West Point from 1852 to 1855 when he was superintendent of the academy. There they might have had occasion to stand in his cool presence to explain some prank, and to squirm under his familiar admonition that an honest man needs but one excuse.

Others, of the older crowd, had observed him with admiration and envy in Mexico where his extraordinary engineering and staff work had won him three brevets to the rank of colonel, and General Scott's lasting esteem.

Then there was the 2nd Cavalry group now with the army, former members of that elite regiment the then Secretary of War Davis had formed in western Texas in 1857 and stocked with the most promising officers in the regular army, most of them Southerners. Lee had been lieutenant colonel of the crack unit and quite a few of the officers who had served under him were in his camps now, including his rollicking twenty-six-year-old nephew, Fitzhugh Lee.

Many had cause to be alarmed at the announcement that it was Lee who would succeed Johnston. Those were the men whose weaknesses and shortcomings the new commander had long ago detected; he had a long memory, even for those he met only briefly. Soon after his appointment, when the matter of the promotion to major general of an officer named Richard H. Anderson came up, Lee advised President Davis in his restrained way:

"I know little of General Anderson personally except as captain of dragoons. He was a favorite in his regiment and was considered a good officer. I am told he is now under a pledge of abstinence which I hope will protect him from the vice he fell into."[7]

Lee had little patience with heavy drinkers and rarely advanced a man who showed too much fondness for the bottle, as his subalterns soon found. To a member of his staff he confided, "I cannot consent to place in the control of others one who cannot control himself."[8]

With Lee now at the helm, many "old service" officers would find themselves frozen at comparatively low rank in the Confederate Army while their juniors passed them, the most humiliating thing that could happen to a professional soldier. Friends and relatives at home in North Carolina or Alabama would be at a loss to explain why the major or lieutenant colonel with all his training and experience was not being advanced. But the subject could generally trace his predicament to some dated incident or encounter with Lee, and could only hope for a new chance in this new service from the man he had failed to favorably impress in the old.

Conversely, others who had done their duty under Lee's eye but could not be rewarded in that promotion-restricted standing army that had only 1,500 officers on its rolls, now looked hopefully to the man for new opportunities and the recognition and advancement which they had long been denied. Actually, nothing better could have happened to the majority of the West Pointers than Lee's gaining command of the army in this still formative stage. For he, more than any other Southern leader, was determined that for as long as possible the key posts were to be held by formally trained professionals. It was a policy that would lead to intense bitterness within his officer corps, but one to which he adhered adamantly.

From the beginning, the academy clique had assumed that control of the army belonged to it almost as a matter of right; but there was no inclination on the part of the dilettante military leaders from civilian life to be left out of the saga of the Confederacy's struggle for independence—particularly when most thought it would be such a brief, one-sided affair. Gladly they relinquished the chores of instructing the recruits to the West Point drillmasters, but they had no desire to see all the glory of the anticipated battlefield triumphs captured by them. There was too much political hay to be made. Scores of public figures—former members of the U. S. Senate and House of Representatives, delegates to the secession conventions, ex-governors and ambitious local officials—managed to gain commissions as colonels and above, frequently by organizing their own regiments.

The landed gentry, the cavaliers from the plantations, men of immense wealth and holdings such as Wade Hampton of South Carolina and Turner Ashby of Virginia, formed another category of leaders that expected to play the same role in the army that they had in dominating the counties from which they had come. Riding forth at the head of great family bands to defend their "way of life," trailed by hordes of black servants carrying their baggage, they approached the war as something out of a Sir Walter Scott novel.

To the amateurs, the West Pointers they encountered had an unwarranted aloofness and made too much show and

ritual of this business of war. To the schooled officers, the
untrained leaders were a worthless set of bombastic orators
and stuffy aristocrats who should have simply stepped aside
when they had finished their work of starting the war, and let
men who knew the game play it out. One sharp-tongued
regular from Virginia rudely called the political general in
whose command he served "as incapacitated for the work he
had undertaken as I would have been to lead an Italian op-
era."[9]

Conversely, an intelligent Georgia lawyer-turned-colo-
nel moaned, "Let me but get away from these West Pointers.
They are very sociable gentlemen and agreeable compan-
ions but never have I seen men who had so little appreciation
of merit in others. Self-sufficiency and self-aggrandizement
are their great controlling characteristics."[10]

Just what special value was there in having attended the
academy anyway? the outsiders asked smugly.

"Take a boy of 16 from his mother's apron strings, shut
him up under constant surveillance for four years at West
Point, send him out to a two-company post upon the frontier
where he does little but play seven-up and drink whiskey at
the sutler's, and by the time he is 45 he will furnish the most
complete illustration of suppressed mental development of
which human nature is capable," concluded one of those
unhappy associates of the academy men.[11]

Even the press was not universally awed by the academy
bunch, particularly during the long period of idleness following the battle of First Manassas on July 21, 1861 when the
leaders of both sides decided their troops needed a great deal
more discipline and drill before they were committed to
battle again.

"The great fault of our campaigns thus far has been that
our generals would not fight their men often enough," the
Richmond *Examiner* editorialized in November 1861. "The
chief thing taught at West Point is mathematics and fortifications and our officers have constantly committed the mistake
of keeping the men busy with their spades, instead of with

their bayonets and muskets, and of being more solicitous of displaying their own mathematical accomplishments than of their soldiers' prowess. We have left West Point at the North on the bleak banks of the Hudson, and we ought to leave West Point tactics to be illustrated by McClellan with his cowardly Yankee and foreign soldiers, more fit for service at the spade than with the musket."[12]

A political general who seemed to delight in ridiculing the West Pointers—even after the fiasco at First Manassas had demonstrated how much their knowledge and guidance were needed—was the man they called "Extra Billy" Smith. A congenial gentleman of sixty-five who had been governor of Virginia, a California gold rusher, and operator of a mail service that imposed so many extra charges it earned him his nickname, Smith now found himself a brigadier general. He hardly looked the part, though, when he was riding along at the head of his troops holding a blue cotton parasol over his head to shield himself from the sun. Smith enjoyed his new military position in every respect except when it came to dealing with the regulars, whom he called "West P'inters" behind their backs and "Mister" to their faces, regardless of rank, merely to infuriate them.

At Seven Pines, Extra Billy's command (a good one, by the way) had been ordered to hold its fire as it advanced but soon came under the torment of sharpshooters concealed in a thicket. His Virginians appealed to Smith for permission to open up on them but the ersatz commander needed no entreaty.

"Of course you can't stand it, boys," he burst out. "It's all this infernal tactics and West Point tomfoolery. Damn it, fire, and flush the game!"[13]

In time, once the incompetents of both factions were weeded out, part of the blind prejudice between the two classes of officers would dissolve but total acceptance would never be achieved. There did develop, instead, tacit recognition that they needed one another. For one thing, there simply were not nearly enough formally trained officers

available to fill all the commands being created. It was up to
the West Pointers to train in their duties not only men in the
lower ranks but the volunteer captains and lieutenants as
well. The latter could not have functioned without the guidance of the professionals. Indeed, few of the volunteers had
any appreciation whatever of what was involved in maintain-
ing a regiment of soldiers in the field. The realization was
abrupt and the consequences exhausting.

"It was my duty not only to make myself comfortable but
a whole Reg't of men," the colonel of the 6th South Carolina
wrote, as he started to catalogue the myriad responsibilities
of his office. It was a list that included "raking up old tents,
building huts, trying to get shoes and blankets, keeping the
camp in good order and all the while drilling and inspecting
and being reviewed and mustering, pay rolls, monthly and
quarterly returns, returns of deceased soldiers and many
other things too numerous to mention."

"It has been," he concluded, "one protracted, head-
cracking job for me."[14]

In many instances, the professionals were forced to admit that some men had a knack for command and could
become effective officers even without formal training, by
diligently applying their intelligence and personalities. In a
Texas regiment, a lawyer named Carter seemed to possess
the gift of knowing how to explain every maneuver set down
in the drill manual so thoroughly and simply that the biggest
blockhead in the ranks could understand them. Unfortunately, he was not strong and the long marches were sometimes too much for him. To help him along, the boys would
divide up his luggage, one taking his sword and belt, another
his haversack and canteen, someone else his blanket; and by
this means he managed to keep up.[15]

Ironically, the training manual the entire army was using—*Rifle and Light Infantry Tactics*—was written in 1853
by William J. Hardee, a member of the West Point class of
1838 who had gone on to serve as instructor of artillery and
cavalry tactics at the academy and as commandant of cadets,

before joining Lee and the 2nd Cavalry in Texas as a lieutenant colonel. If the Confederates wished amplification of any point mentioned in his text they had merely to approach him directly, for Hardee too was in the Rebel camp.

In a driving rainstorm, a minor engagement took place at Chantilly, Virginia, during the summer campaign of 1862. At one point the medley of lightning and thunder, rifle fire and shouting panicked the horse being ridden by the Federal General Philip Kearny, and the animal galloped out of control toward the Confederate lines. Kearny, a one-armed daredevil of a fighter known throughout the regular army, was riddled by Southern marksmen. After the battle ended, his drenched, mud-sullied body was recovered by the Rebels and taken to the porch of a rundown cabin.

When General A. P. Hill of Virginia, who had been acquainted with the fallen Union officer for many years, arrived and saw the disheveled form, he lamented, "Poor Kearny, he deserved a better death than that."[16]

The staff members around the little Confederate leader no doubt thought it strange that their commander was so touched by the death of an enemy officer. They did not yet understand the feelings that these "old army" men from both camps would continue to hold for one another. Theirs was to be a separate relationship, uninfluenced by the feelings of the men they led. It was Lee himself who had a truce arranged in order to return Kearny's body to his lines, and who personally saw to it that his sword and other private belongings were returned to the dead general's wife in New Jersey.

Even when the war reached its grimmest stages, there would be no hatred among the professionals. Ties were too strong among these men who not only knew each other by their first names but had long ago crowned one another with special sobriquets that people outside of the army had never heard. Confederate cavalry leader James Ewell Brown Stuart might be known as "Jeb" throughout the Rebel army, but to the army men who knew him before the war he would always be "Beauty" or just "Beaut"—not because he was so good looking but because he was not. For some unexplained incident, Henry Walker had won the name "Mud" from the class of 1853 and it stayed with him throughout his frontier service with the 6th Infantry. If he thought that advancement to the lofty rank of brigadier general in the Confederate Army would finally relieve him of the undignified appellation, he was embarrassingly disappointed on more than one occasion when he encountered an old chum. When they talked of the enemy commanders, it was not "Billy" Sherman, as the privates in the ranks called William Tecumseh Sherman, but "Cump" and, of course, Ulysses S. Grant was called "Sam."

So little animosity existed between the officer corps of the two armies that in one instance we find Dick Ewell, the bald-headed dragoon, confidently advising his middle-aged fiancée as the Yankees approached her Tennessee home:

"Take away your Negroes, and leave some trusty whites in your house with letters to Grant, Buell, or Thomas, or Sherman—to all of whom you might say I referred you."[17]

After First Manassas, General James Longstreet had to politely turn down an invitation to dinner extended by his old friend, General Israel Richardson of the Union Army. The host was disappointed at the rejection though Longstreet tried to explain that Richardson must be more careful lest the politicians have him arrested for giving aid and comfort to the enemy.[18]

The guards at Libby Prison were taken aback when the commander of the Texas Brigade—John Bell Hood—showed up one morning at the Richmond tobacco warehouse and asked to see two of their prisoners, Union officers Whiting and Chambliss. What business did the general have with the captured Yankee bigwigs? the guards wondered, but it is doubtful that they asked the booming-voiced brigadier or that he bothered to explain that he had served with both men in Texas and he was concerned about their welfare.[19]

During this same period, a party of Federal officers, firm friends of Colonel "Shanks" Evans, a great favorite in the old days, showed up before the Confederate lines under a flag of truce and lugging a basket that turned out to be filled with champagne bottles. Hours later they returned, much less laden, after a noisy frolic behind the flaps of Colonel Evans' tent.[20]

Following that initial battle at Manassas, Jeb Stuart also went to the front and met many of his classmates and friends with the Federal army. One of them produced a "basket of nice things" and the group proceeded to picnic in a shady spot in the neutral zone between the lines. "It was amusing to hear them talking of their exploits on opposite sides in the battle," an eavesdropping orderly remembered.[21]

Understandably enough, General Pickett had difficulty making his young sweetheart appreciate this peculiar link the regulars maintained in an atmosphere of disunion. In one letter he wrote from the works around Richmond, he made mention of his supposed adversary, George McClellan:

"He was, he is and he always will be even were his pistol pointed at my heart, my dear, loved friend. You, my darling, may not be in sympathy with this feeling, for I know you see 'no good in Nazareth'. . . . You cannot understand the entente cordiale between us old fellows."[22]

Union General Ambrose Burnside was a particular favorite among the Confederates and, curiously, the fact that it was he who had suffered at their hands the awful defeat at Fredericksburg was genuinely disturbing to them. A genial, open, warm-hearted man, Burnside had never sought command of the army, tried to turn it down when it was thrust upon him, and relinquished it as soon as he was permitted. No one knew better than Burnside himself that he did not have the ability to command an army. When the hopelessly one-sided battle was over, Pickett, himself destined for a colossal failure, confided to his fiancée, "I can't help feeling sorry for old Burnside, proud, plucky, hard-headed old dog. I always liked him."[23]

Certainly as upset was Confederate Harry Heth, who had been Burnside's roommate at West Point. Never was there a more ill-advised pairing for both were incorrigible pranksters. A favorite routine called for Harry to intercept arriving plebes, inform them that regulations required they have their hair cropped within twenty-four hours, and forthwith escort them to Room 111. There Ambrose, with sheet and scissors, awaited the customers and proceeded to give their heads the most grotesque shearings he and Harry could devise.[24]

Burnside could never stay out of mischief. In Mexico he gambled so heavily his pay was spent for years to come. One of his poker creditors apparently was A. P. Hill because at Fredericksburg, when someone asked Powell, as his friends called him, if he knew Burnside, he replied tersely, "Ought to, he owes me $8,000."[25]

On the heights above the Rappahannock, Burnside had gotten into the biggest trouble of his life and this time none of the legion of chums who loved him could do anything to console him. There was no bringing back those thousands of fallen Union soldiers. A Confederate officer who met Burnside after the battle under a flag of truce, to arrange for the burial of the dead, found him terribly mortified and distressed. After they had talked for an hour in a friendly vein, the shaken Burnside thoughtfully wrapped up a bottle of brandy for the staff officer to take back. With it, though, came a request for a favor. For the sake of his reputation, Ambrose asked the young officer "to tell his old army friends on the other side that he was not responsible for the attack on Fredericksburg in the manner in which it was made, as he was himself under orders."[26]

Time and time again throughout the conflict, the "old fellows" would be suddenly reminded of their former relationship by unexpected encounters under the strangest of circumstances. Cadmus Wilcox, the jumpy little brigadier the men called Old Billy Fixing, was moving forward at the head of his brigade across the battlefield at Second Manassas that was still littered with dead and wounded. He noticed a short distance away a handkerchief being waved weakly by a limp, prone figure in blue. Cadmus left the column, trotted over to the signaler, and discovered he was a Federal general, an old classmate, who had recognized him and desired to say farewell. When the man expired, Wilcox took personal responsibility for caring for the body.[27]

During one battle, Union General George Armstrong Custer ordered his men not to fire on a conspicuous Confederate cavalry leader wearing a scarlet-lined cape. The next day, under a flag of truce, Custer sent a message through the lines addressed to his former classmate from Texas, General Thomas Rosser, that read, "Tam, do not expose yourself so. Yesterday I could have killed you."[28]

Some members of the academy clique were, naturally, more popular than others. Some, in fact, were heartily disliked at the school and out on the frontier, and the changed circumstances did nothing to alter these attitudes. Two Confederate generals were captured together in the Union breakthrough at Spotsylvania—"Allegheny" Ed Johnson, class of '38, and one of his brigadiers, George "Maryland" Steuart, class of '48—and then underwent totally different experiences at the hands of their captors, mainly because of the old days.

Johnson had fought like a madman to avoid capture, swinging a huge staff he carried to support a wounded leg and warding off bayonets until overpowered and disarmed. As he was led off, the gruff division commander was extremely humiliated at being taken and kept coughing to hide his emotion. Generals Meade and Grant saw him passing to the rear and intercepted Johnson to shake hands with him and see that he was not abused. General A. S. Williams was even more considerate. He took him away from his guards and marched him off to breakfast at his own mess.[29]

General Steuart, on the other hand, insulted everybody who came near him. He chose the wrong man when he tried his surliness on Union General Winfield Scott Hancock. The

Second Corps commander knew Steuart and courteously extended his hand when he encountered the captive.

"How are you, Steuart?" he asked.

"Under the circumstances I decline to take your hand," was the reply.

Hancock shot back, "And under any other circumstances I should not have offered it."[30]

The irritating "little creature" was rewarded for his manner by being sent on foot to Fredericksburg by a route that had him alternately sloshing through mud and crossing streams as deep as his waist.

As might be imagined, there were many strong friendships between the West Pointers' wives as well, and the women found various ways to keep in touch while their husbands fought one another. There was a good deal of traffic between North and South throughout the war and notes could be passed or messages conveyed by travelers.

Even General McClellan's wife, the former Ellen Marcy, daughter of a West Pointer and regular army officer, kept in touch with acquaintances across the Potomac. She was delighted in one instance to receive a smuggled letter from a lady friend in Richmond telling her:

"I have seen at different times many of your old army friends, General A. P. Hill, Edward Johnson, and many others, and I assure you 'Miss Nellie,' as they still call you, is often spoken of."[31]

Powell Hill! How vividly she could remember those days when she had both him and George McClellan wooing her, and when she had finally decided on the latter, with a bit of nudging from her father. What she did not know was that the rumor-rampant camps of both the army in blue and the one in gray had become well aware of that romantic rivalry. Now whenever McClellan and Hill came up against one another and a battle was imminent, the men of both sides moaned, "My God, Nellie Marcy, why didn't you marry him?"[32]

3

The Leaders

THE SEVEN DAYS, that awful period in June 1862 when five bloody battles were fought by Lee to drive the Army of the Potomac from the outskirts of the Confederate capital, was the crucible of the Army of Northern Virginia.

It was that week of constant, desperate warfare that forged the army's character, gave it cohesion, provided it with the opportunity to experience its powers and gain confidence in itself and in its leader.

Gaines Mill . . . Frayser's Farm . . . Mechanicsville . . . Malvern Hill . . . almost every day an awesome struggle as the Confederates, outnumbered but taking the offensive, pressed McClellan back out of sight of the spires of Richmond while the city's inhabitants filled their homes with the wounded. How an officer demonstrated he could handle great masses of troops on the difficult, often swampy terrain; that he could make intelligent decisions with the terribly fragmented information available to him, keep his head in spite of the uproar and din that seemed never to diminish, and control nerves jangled by days with little or no sleep, determined his place in this army. It was here that the chaff was winnowed from the wheat. It was here that the true leaders emerged.

Men who in the quiet first year of the war had made excellent military reputations for themselves, campaigning in the ballrooms and theatre lobbies of Richmond or the crowded bars of the bustling Stafford and Spotswood hotels, were suddenly deflated when they were called upon to control large units in actual combat. Many of those detected as too excitable, too dull, too old, or too timid to be trusted in responsible positions again were men of lofty rank and strong social position and were by no means willing to admit their failings. But in moves that were masterpieces of tact and diplomacy, Lee managed to get rid of virtually every man he desired. No one was cashiered or overly humiliated. All were simply transferred to quiet sectors and given imposing but meaningless titles to satisfy their pride.

When the campaign was over, Lee had decided on the organization that would best suit the officer corps he had to work with and the topography of the theatre of war in which he had to perform. Breaking up the unwieldy grand divisions he had inherited from Joe Johnston, he created two infantry corps—the first under Lieutenant General James Longstreet and the second commanded by Lieutenant General Thomas J. Jackson. Each would be composed of four infantry divisions —units that would average four brigades each and total roughly 7,000 men each. The cavalry would be headed by Major General Jeb Stuart.

Solid, dependable were the words that first came to mind in describing Longstreet, the stocky Georgian the men from the old service called "Dutch" and "Old Pete." Though it would become clear that Lee had more respect for the military intellect of the strange, enigmatic Jackson than for Longstreet's cerebral abilities, he would gradually become more and more attached to Longstreet personally. He could converse more freely with him and obviously enjoyed his company. There was a coolness about this former Fort Leavenworth paymaster, who was 40 at the start of the war, that was comforting and assuring. An observant Englishman serving with the Confederates once studied Longstreet in the field and left this image of the man outside a farmhouse headquarters:

"Longstreet sat in an old garden chair at the foot of the steps under shady trees, busily engaged in disposing of a lunch of sandwiches. With his feet thrown against a tree, he presented a true type of the hardy campaigner; his once gray uniform had changed to brown and many a button was missing; his riding boots were dusty and worn but his pistols and sabre had a bright polish by his side while his charger stood near, anxiously looking at him.

"Though the day was warm, the general's coat was buttoned up and as he ate and conversed with those about him, it was evident that his sandy beard, moustache and half bald head had lately but distant dealings with a barber. He was a little above medium height, thick set, inclined to obesity and has a small inquiring blue eye. Though thoughtful and slow of motion he is remarkably industrious."[1]

Longstreet's great talent was an incredible ability to handle large bodies of men in action. During the Seven Days, Major Moxley Sorrel, the man who was probably closest to Longstreet throughout the war, observed he "had held his men, as it were, in the hollow of his hand." To his young chief of staff, Longstreet "was like a rock of steadiness when sometimes in battle the world seemed flying to pieces."[2]

Longstreet gradually became something of a father image to his men. He was looked upon as a firm, indestructible, imperturbable leader whom his boys felt would take the best possible care of them in camp, on the march, and in battle. There was very little color about him. Neither a brilliant nor a clever conversationalist, he was, in fact, quite taciturn; and even more so after a dreadful personal tragedy befell him during the first year of the war, the loss of three of his children in Richmond during a scarlet fever epidemic.

He was an earthy man. He drank and sometimes quite

heavily. ("Please send the General some more of your peach brandy," a young soldier wrote his father. "It is about half gone. General Longstreet took to it amazingly."[3])

He was stubborn, deliberate, and often downright slow, exasperating traits even to such a model of patience as Lee.

"He was the hardest man to move that I had under me," Marse Robert lamented. But Longstreet's overriding feature was that he was a man who knew what he was doing: the seasoned, experienced soldier in full control of the situation.[4]

The men under Thomas J. "Stonewall" Jackson were not long in discovering that they were in the hands of a most odd and eccentric individual, and they could readily understand why the Virginia Military Institute men among them had nicknamed their old instructor "Tom Fool" Jackson.

His dress was pathetic, invariably consisting of a faded blue coat, a battered, flopping *kepi* with its visor drawn low over the brow, dusty hip-length boots of giant size. An awkward horseman, he generally appeared off balance and on the verge of toppling out of the saddle. One private in the ranks, not recognizing the officer he saw being tossed about by his horse, once went up to him and inquired where he had found the liquor.

He was an uncommunicative, wooden-faced man of many peculiar habits of which the least unusual was that of seeming always to be sucking on a lemon. Religious to the extreme, he would avoid having a battle on Sunday whenever possible and would frequently halt what he was doing and slip into his tent for prayer when the meditative mood seized him.

Probably the most frustrating of Jackson's traits for the officers who had to serve him was his secretiveness, often carried to the point of absurdity. He would march his troops madly about in all directions, frequently making them retrace their steps for miles, telling not even his brigade commanders their ultimate destination or the purpose of the trek. He confided in no one. When Jackson began to bring them victories, the members of his "foot cavalry" were willing to allow him his unorthodox ways; but in the beginning they were convinced they were serving a madman and a cold, unfeeling one at that.

Those closest to Stonewall were able to see that he followed certain military practices unswervingly. His prime rule was "always mystify, mislead and surprise the enemy, if possible, and when you strike and overcome him, never let up in the pursuit as long as your men have strength to follow."[5] Another principle he lived by was "never fight against heavy odds if by any possible maneuvering you can hurl your own force on only a part, and that the weakest part of your enemy and crush it. Such tactics will win every time and a small army may thus destroy a large one in detail."[6]

How he applied these dictums—from the Shenandoah Valley to Chancellorsville—would be studied at military schools and army staff colleges around the world a century after he was gone.

Only the toughest, most determined volunteers could keep up with Jackson. Even as rugged a soldier as Dorsey Pender of the First Dragoons complained bitterly that "Jackson forgets that one gets tired, hungry or sleepy" and, at another time, that "Stonewall" would "kill up the army the way he marches."[7] Pathetically comical was an appeal the surgeon of the 34th North Carolina sent to Governor Zeb Vance for a transfer home, because "in the state service I imagine the troops will be mostly stationary and will not have a Stonewall Jackson to march after."[8] One winter's service convinced a horse artilleryman named Neese that he had had all he desired of "Stonewall's Way."

"That little old faded cap that General Jackson wears may shelter a brain that is filled with skeletons of strategic maneuvers, war maps and battlefield plans," he wrote. "But if he thinks that we are India rubber and can keep on courting death with impunity by marching in the snow with wet feet all day and then be snowed under at night, he will find that by the time the robins sing again half his command will be in the hospital or answering roll call in some other clime."[9]

One of Jackson's brigadiers, Lawton of Georgia, went more to the essence of his commander: "He was a one-idea man. He looked upon the broken-down men and stragglers as the same thing. He classed all who were weak or weary, who fainted by the wayside, as men wanting in patriotism. If a man's face was as white as cotton and his pulse so low you scarce could feel it, he looked upon him merely as an inefficient soldier and rode off impatiently. Like all the successful warriors of the world he did not value human life where he had an object to accomplish. He could order men to their death as a matter of course. His soldiers obeyed him to the death. Faith they had in him stronger than death. Their respect he commanded. I doubt if he had so much of their love."[10]

As distinctly different as were Longstreet and Jackson from one another, so were the division commanders of the two corps. In the First Corps, three of the four major generals —Lafayette McLaws, George Pickett, and Richard H. Anderson—were of the steady, reliable, loyal subordinate sort, experienced and seasoned but without any great spark or inspirational quality. There was no natural combativeness in their makeup that could be suddenly inflamed by the sound of the guns, nor any degree of infectious energy and spirit about them. The fourth division commander of Longstreet's corps —John Bell Hood—was everything the others were not.

McLaws of Georgia was a boyhood friend of Longstreet's as well as a West Point classmate. He shared Old Pete's careful, deliberate ways and could be as painstakingly slow. He exhibited this at Sharpsburg when (despite an order from Lee that the utmost despatch was required) he failed to bring his division back from the Harpers Ferry foray until hours after the army leaders thought he could have rejoined.

"He certainly could not be called an intellectual man, nor was he brilliant and aggressive," a man who knew

McLaws well concluded, "but he was regarded as one of the most dogged defensive fighters in the army. His entire makeup, physical, mental and moral was solid. He was short, stout, square-shouldered, deep-chested and strong limbed. In complexion, he was dark and swarthy, with coal black eyes and thick close-curling hair and beard. Of his type, he was a handsome man, but his type was that of a Roman centurion—say that centurion who stood at his post in Herculaneum until the lava ran over him."[11]

When he cared to be, McLaws could be a dandy dresser and a familiar photograph of him shows the division commander wearing a splendid cape, a French kepi beautifully embroidered, and trousers sporting a broad infantry stripe. Morale was always high in his command. He maintained it by mixing intimately and good-naturedly with his troops and his chunky figure mounted on a small white pony was a familiar sight in the camps.

A 6th Infantry captain in the old days, McLaws had seen much hard service even before the Mexican War broke out. He experienced a good deal of action south of the border and when that conflict was over he ran into more harrowing duty escorting wagon trains to California. When the Civil War began, he had just returned from a long expedition against the Navajos in New Mexico.

Dick Anderson, like McLaws and Longstreet, was a man in his early forties during the war years and was also a member of that historic West Point class of 1842 that furnished thirty-two general officers to the Union and Confederate armies. If Sorrel had him sized up accurately (and the supporting evidence is substantial) Anderson was an extremely brave leader but of a rather inert, indolent manner, by no means pushy or aggressive. Anderson's capacity and intelligence were excellent but, Sorrel found, "it was hard to get him to use them."[12] Longstreet knew Anderson—a short, stocky figure with a very agreeable face—extremely well from the old days and could get a good deal out of him.

A retiring, contemplative, modest type of man, Anderson was of good family, born on a Sumter County, South Carolina plantation. Most of his prewar service had been with the Second Dragoons, in which he was a captain. Aside from the emotional conflict of fighting against men from his old unit, he had to bear an even more personal one for he was married to the daughter of the chief justice of Pennsylvania, a young lady he had met and wooed while serving as a cavalry instructor at Carlisle Barracks. Naturally, Lee never questioned his loyalty but he did have his eye on Anderson on another account, as has been indicated. He remembered him at Fort Kearny, Nebraska, as an officer who drank too much.

Longstreet's fondness for George Pickett was difficult to fathom. Pickett—showy, affected, seeming always to be taking far better care of himself than his men—could not have been more unlike Longstreet, who had known him since Mexico; but Dutch had a liking for George. In sending orders to Pickett in the field, Longstreet made sure his staff officers conveyed things very explicitly and, indeed, sometimes made them stay with Pickett to make sure he did not go astray.[13]

Pickett, the white-gloved inspector, was a man in his late thirties and about five years younger than the class of '42 alumnus. He too was an old army captain who had done much of his service in the Pacific Northwest (once lending his flag and uniform to a harebrained scheme to provoke a border incident with British authorities in the hope of creating an international crisis that might distract the nation from its civil war course).

Though he may have failed to sustain it, Pickett did make a striking first impression on people merely by his appearance, or more specifically his coiffure. He was of only medium size, straight and erect, but the head—that is, the hair—was extraordinary. Long, perfumed ringlets flowed loosely over his shoulders. His beard also was curly and gave out the scents of Araby. In fact, George was known everywhere by his corkscrew ringlets which, alas, as milady's, were not particularly becoming when he was caught in the rain and they went lank.

Hood, commander of an amalgamated force of troops from various states which was sometimes called the Texas Division because of the three crack Texas regiments in the unit, was distinctly different from the other First Corps division commanders. A man of imposing presence—tall, blond-bearded, with a voice that resounded with authority—Hood was as rugged as any of the fierce fighters serving under him. He was one of the 2nd Cavalry boys who had come to the Confederate Army out of Fort Mason with Lee, and already had some reputation with the Texas volunteers as an Indian fighter in their home state, a fact that had made him immediately acceptable to them.

A Kentucky physician's son, Hood—called "Sam" by his friends—was an aggressive, driving person on the battlefield, as a social climber in Richmond, and in the military council. A soldier in the ranks, who admired him greatly, detected the essential flaw in the man:

"Hood was ambitious as he was brave and daring . . . like Henry of the Wynl in the combat between the clans . . . he fought for his own hand."[14]

His great successes at Gaines Mill and Second Manassas, where he had launched line-crushing attacks of enormous ferocity, and the fight he had made at Sharpsburg in the cornfield were widely publicized and Hood had rapidly become the model of every wooden gun–toting boy in Richmond and the coveted beau of every unattached belle who hadn't lost her heart to Jeb Stuart.

The key leaders of Jackson's Second Corps—A. P. Hill, Dick Ewell, and Daniel Harvey Hill—were of a different sort than Longstreet's subalterns, generally of a more fiery, pugnacious nature which they were able to convey to their men. They seemed of a tougher, more warlike mold and, when they deemed it necessary, could drive their troops hard and fight them until they bled white.

The personal bravery of each was inspiring. All exposed themselves freely and deliberately in the hottest contests. Ewell often went forward with the skirmishers.

Ewell, the hard-swearing dragoon captain who averred that in two decades of service he had learned all about caring for fifty dragoons and forgotten everything else about being an officer, was a man of no ordinary appearance. He had bright, prominent eyes, a bomb-shaped bald head, and a nose like Francis of Valois which gave him a striking resemblance to a woodcock. The impression was increased by his habit of putting his head on one side before lisping his droll and witty, occasionally intolerant and usually profane speeches.

Ewell wore fierce grizzled mustaches sticking up and out like a terrier and had peculiarities of behavior to match his physical oddities. He fancied he suffered some mysterious internal malady and would eat nothing but frementy, a wheat preparation; he developed a plaintive way of talking of his disease, almost as if he were someone else. His nervousness prevented his taking regular sleep and he passed nights curled around a camp stool in positions that would dislocate an ordinary person's joints.

After a few weeks with Jackson in the Shenandoah, even this strange man (who kept an Apache boy he had brought back from the Southwest in his camp as a servant and companion)[15] was confiding that he "admired his genius but was certain of his lunacy."[16] Ewell admitted that he "never saw one of Jackson's couriers approaching without expecting an order to assault the North Pole."[17]

In a letter to a relative, the peppery subaltern complained, "I have a bad headache, what with the bother and folly of things. I never suffered so much from dyspepsia in my life. As an Irishman would say 'I'm kilt entirely.' "[18]

Despite Ewell's outward flap, Jackson was impressed with the way the old dragoon could fight troops. He also liked the military maxim he had heard attributed to him, the rule that held "the road to glory can't be followed with much baggage."[19]

A. P. Hill, a proud, slender, auburn-bearded Virginian warmly regarded by both his officers and enlisted men, was rather dandified in his dress with the insignia of his rank usually conspicuous amidst the gold braid and brass buttons. He was a stylish horseman, always well mounted, and, all in all, presented a very graceful appearance.

His associates thought of him as alert, bold, and skillful in battle, though some might substitute the word "impetuous" for alert. If Lee had any concern over Hill's rashness, his tendency to rush into things, he gave no hint of it to President Davis when he advised him that after Longstreet and Jackson, "I consider A. P. Hill the best commander with me. He fights his troops well and takes good care of them."[20]

The battles of the Seven Days had demonstrated that Hill was not squeamish about casualties and would not hesitate to take frightful losses if he felt a victory could be secured by the effort. But Powell, West Point '47 and for 14 years a 1st Artillery lieutenant, was no butcher and amply showed to his men his sincere personal regard for them by the way he concerned himself with their needs. He fought for them between campaigns as they fought for him in battle. Despite its huge size, nearly 12,000 men, his Light Division was one of the most close-knit, smooth-running units in the army.

If there was a fault in the refined, gentlemanly makeup of A. P. Hill, it was a certain oversensitivity, that inclination to overreact to real or imagined slights from his superiors. "General Hill is a brave officer but perhaps too quick to resent seeming overstepping of authority," Jed Hotchkiss, Jackson's keen-eyed topographical engineer, observed about him.[21] It may have been the vice of pride but if he sensed that he was being abused by his commanders, put down in any way, he quickly boiled over and stubbornly demanded amends. Longstreet, who did not like Powell and had already encountered this streak, thought there was a good deal of "curled darling and dress parade" about him.[22]

For sheer fearlessness, D. H. (Harvey) Hill could not be

rivaled. So often did he place his life in danger that he himself took the step of preparing his wife (the sister of Stonewall Jackson's second wife) for what most certainly would be his fate when he wrote, "You have been living a widow's life for nearly a year now and you may soon be a widow in fact."[23]

A singular individual indeed was Harvey Hill. He had quit the army in 1849, partly for the sake of his new bride, after attending West Point and serving in Mexico.

"I cannot contemplate without horror her entrance into one of our wretched garrisons," he confided before turning to the academic life.[24] Religious to a degree that equaled the devoutness of his brother-in-law, Hill wrote scholarly works on biblical subjects before the war and his fervor became more intense when the conflict was joined.

"When I ride along the ranks and hear the gross profanity and vulgarity of the soldiers, I cannot wonder at our reverses," the pious combat leader would lament.[25] Hill was every bit as offensive in speech as in military tactics, his critical, scathing manner nurtured no doubt by the constant, excruciating pain he had suffered since boyhood from a spinal injury.

A Union general responsible for some depredations in North Carolina late in the war got a strong dose of Harvey Hill's sometimes startling language when the Federal leader found himself cut off and asked for surrender terms. Hill replied: "The officers and men under your command will be treated as prisoners of war, but you will be castrated."[26]

In spite of (or, perhaps, because of) their family relationship, Stonewall Jackson carried on practically no personal rapport with Hill, who thought it strange but apparently did not let it disturb him. In a letter to his wife, he simply said of her brother, "His correspondence is strictly official; it's a funny world."[27]

The fourth division of the Second Corps, the "Stonewall Division" as it was called because it was Jackson's original command, did not have a regular commander for a long time until Edward Johnson rejoined the army after Chancellorsville. Until then, except for Jackson, all of its leaders had fallen in grim succession in the first battle under their command. At Sharpsburg, General Starke, only in temporary command in place of the wounded 'permanent' commanding officer, was killed before word could even be passed to the men in the ranks of his appointment.

The man succeeding to this precarious post was a rough, bulky old soldier who had been wounded the year before while earning his nickname by stubbornly defending the mountain passes during Jackson's Valley Campaign. Johnson's damaged foot was still not fully healed and to help bolster his sizeable form he had taken to carrying a long hickory pole that (in an army where any peculiarity brought wild hoots and hollers from the men in the ranks) fairly caused an uproar when first he brandished it. Now they called him "Fence Rail" Johnson because of the crutch which one artilleryman remembered as being as long as a rail and almost as thick as the club of Giant Despair.

Though he was greeted with jeers by the troops who did not recognize him, those who knew his record realized that the army was gaining, through Johnson's return to duty, a solid, high-calibre offer with twenty-five years of active field duty that included battling Seminoles in Florida, participation in all of the great encounters in Mexico from Cerro Gordo to Chapultepec, and long service at such hazardous frontier posts as Fort Riley, Kansas, and Fort Laramie, Dakota Territory.

Aside from the crutch he carried, probably the most pronounced oddity about the forty-seven-year-old Virginian was the shape of his head, which resembled something of a triple tiara. Mrs. Mary B. Chesnut, a social leader who saw him often in Richmond where he was also a favorite, thought his strongly shaped dome was "like a cone on an old fashioned beehive." She also noted that he seemed to be persistently winking one eye at her but he was not flirting. In Mexico, he had been wounded in the eye and the nerve vibrated independently.

Continuing with his imperfections, Mrs. Chesnut pointed out that he was somewhat hard of hearing and consequently spoke in a loud, roaring voice which she said often caused embarrassment when the old bachelor was courting ladies in Richmond drawing rooms.[28]

A large and rather rough-looking man, Ed was never particular about his dress and he was observed one day looking rough indeed with some of his rather scanty, sandy-colored hair sticking through a rent in his old slouch hat. If he was wearing his usual ensemble, Johnson probably also had on a long frock coat—and could not care less how unregulation he appeared.

Jeb Stuart, the cavalryman who long ago had aided Lee and the capture of John Brown at Harpers Ferry in an incident whose historic significance neither of them sensed, seemed to daily add to the army's lore with his daring escapades, both military and social, and his D'Artagnan-like dress. A stocky, red-bearded man of boundless, infectious energy, he could accomplish remarkable feats of endurance while rarely showing any signs of fatigue and being always ready to join in if the spirited young officers with whom he surrounded himself were headed for a dance or a charade. The fair sex adored Jeb and his jingling spurs, his plumed hats and satin-lined capes. Wherever he stopped, women draped him with garlands and beseeched him for buttons from his uniform or some other token. Although he dearly loved their attention, there is no evidence that he ever strayed from his wife, who was the daughter, it will be recalled, of the Union General Cooke whose troopers Jeb was now frequently encountering on his spectacular rides around the Union armies. But Stuart was not all play. His squadrons watched the enemy ceaselessly, intercepting couriers, raiding telegraph stations, guarding fords. No Federal leader moved a regiment without word being sent to Lee's headquarters before his unit's campfires were extinguished.

Looking at these lieutenant and major generals who commanded the corps and divisions of the Army of Northern Virginia as a bloc, one may notice that all save Hood and Stuart were men in their late thirties or early and mid-forties, all were West Point–educated and, but for D. H. Hill and Jackson, all had been on active duty in the old army when the war began. Significantly, only one—Longstreet—had risen above the rank of captain, the rank of a company commander.

Despite their common backgrounds, the pronounced differences in appearance, personality, and manner of these men made them anything but a stereotyped group—the intelligent but idle Anderson; the ambitious, forceful Hood; the loud, crusty Ed Johnson; the affected Pickett; the steady, plodding McLaws; the impetuous, touchy A. P. Hill; the puritanical, fearless D. H. Hill; the picturesque, eccentric Ewell; the enigmatic Jackson; the stolid Longstreet; and the fun-loving, romantic Stuart.

What did make them a singular group, however, was the fact that virtually every member, flawed as he may have been, was irreplaceable. In every case where a position became vacant due to death or disability, promotion or transfer, it had to be filled by a lesser man as Lee was forced to progressively compromise his standards and advance some men too far merely to fill the gaps. The army gradually weakened as a result. While this group was substantially intact, the army was at its best.

4

"A Contempt for Danger"

MAJOR GENERAL D. H. HILL of North Carolina, as has been mentioned, was an extremely brave man yet, by no means, a fellow anxious to throw away his life. To members of his staff, however, he appeared bent on doing just that when they observed him, a cigar jutting defiantly from between his clenched teeth, riding the length of his infantry line completely exposed to the fire of the enemy during one of those dreadful battles of the Seven Days around Richmond. When he returned, miraculously unscathed, they pleaded with him not to take such chances.

"I did it for a purpose," he snapped back. "I saw that our men were wavering and I wanted to give them confidence."[1]

Hill was one of the first to recognize the grim truth about what was going to be required to move this newly formed and already pitifully maintained volunteer army. And he was resigned to doing what he knew must be done.

The Southern soldier going into battle required inspiration. The need to uphold the principle of state's rights became less and less compelling to a seventeen-year-old farmboy from Georgia as the number of bluecoats in front of his Enfield rifle seemed to multiply instead of diminish, the longer he stood his ground and fought. There were few professional soldiers around to reassure him, to hold him to his work. At the outset of the war there could not have been a thousand career non-coms in the Confederate ranks.

Example and motivation had to come from a much higher level and from someone in a position to influence large numbers of men at a time in the heat and passion of battle. The responsibility fell to the colonels and brigadiers, the men in command of regiments and brigades. Some couldn't meet the demands on them for public shows of fearlessness and valor and became the first to run off into the woods when the minié balls began whirring by. The men under their command usually were quick to follow.

A South Carolina officer didn't try to conceal his disgust with General Pickett when he encountered him during one of those battles of the Seven Days standing by his horse in a deep, small hollow that looked almost like a well, bewailing himself. He called out for a litter, insisting he was mortally wounded; but the regimental officer, busy with his men, could not be bothered after concluding that "he was very slightly wounded and perfectly able to take care of himself."[2]

Many of the officers were just naturally fearless and combative and had reputations in the old army for their toughness. Dorsey Pender rarely got through a battle unscathed. At Fredericksburg, the young Carolinian was seen riding down his line through a hail of shot and shells, as Harvey Hill had done, his left arm hanging limply at his side with blood streaming down his fingers. At Second Manassas, a shell grazed his skull, an incident he dismissed in a letter to his wife, Fanny, with these words: "My head is well but a little more bald than of yore."[3]

Yet such conduct was no revelation to the officers who knew Pender in the First Dragoons and were well aware of how, as a second lieutenant just out of West Point, he had turned the battle of Spokane Plains in Washington Territory. He did it by galloping up to an Indian chieftain, grabbing him by the arm and throat, and carrying him in that fashion away from his braves and back to his line where he then picked up the warrior and hurled him into the midst of his troopers.[4]

Other officers relied on fiery eloquence, shouting fervent appeals to manhood, patriotism, pride, or duty, whatever would take effect. If entreaty or personal exposure failed and their men, for some reason, just were not up to a fight that day, the Confederate leaders took a different approach. They drew their swords and swung them at their own men, not always using the flat side of the blade. In some cases, an officer cocked his revolver and held the barrel against the skull of a frightened man and gave him one last chance to get up and move forward. It was a side to the war the folks at home did not hear of, conduct never alluded to in those windy, flowery speeches at the dedication of the battlefield monuments much later, but it went on . . . and not infrequently.

What became plain was that few units were willing to let a commander gain a high reputation as a combat leader by risking their lives without endangering his own.

As one Confederate colonel told a foreign observer: "The only way in which an officer could acquire influence over the Confederate soldiers was by his personal conduct under fire. They hold a man in great esteem who in action sets them an example of contempt for danger; but they think nothing of an officer who is not in the habit of leading them. In fact, such a man could not possibly retain his position . . . every atom of authority has to be purchased by a drop of your blood."[5]

Just before the battle of Fredericksburg, a captain of the 21st Georgia engaged in a little facts-of-life talk with a twenty-five-year-old colonel who had just taken command of the regiment.

"Colonel, we dash right into them. We either promote our commanders or get them shot," the captain advised the young officer. "I hear Burnside is crossing the river. If you are the right kind of stuff and will lead, we will make you Brigadier General Hoke tomorrow, or get you killed."

The young colonel listened attentively and, when his advisor was finished, he looked him in the face and replied, "That's the kind of talk I like to hear."[6]

Indeed, it was the type of proposition that would appeal to many of Lee's officers, particularly the regular army crowd. So burning was the ambition of some, an ambition so long stifled in the miniature peacetime army, that they now were ready to unpausingly take the most desperate risks with their lives if, by their shows of daring, they could inspire their men to a victory that would bring the attention and credit to them. It was a foolish but irrepressible urge in so many of the officers who came to Lee's army with the view that it offered an opportunity as well as a noble cause. They believed in state's rights; they were certain that they had no choice but to go to the defense of their invaded states; they wanted to serve the Confederacy but few had any intention of doing so in an anonymous fashion. None were ready to take the obscure positions they had held in Federal service. Men who had spent eight years as lieutenants now chafed at remaining colonels for more than six months. Promotion of an acquaintance who had held a lower rank in the old service was enough for a West Pointer to start generating every degree of political pressure he or his family could stir up in the state capital or in Richmond to gain similar advancement.

Too often these matters which had jealousy, pride, and ambition as their source were brought to Lee to resolve, and he had neither the time nor understanding to cope with them. They were common weaknesses, but to a man who made his entire life a monument to the word "duty," they were strange vices to comprehend.

"It seems General Lee has not patience with any personal complaint or grievance," concluded Mrs. Chesnut, the social leader who had heard many of the plaintiffs discuss their situation in her drawing room. "He is all for the cause."

A typical case of discontent was Cadmus Wilcox, the nervous little commander of an Alabama brigade introduced earlier. Just before Fredericksburg, Wilcox formally re-

quested a transfer to another Confederate army. The war
had been on for only a year and a half but Wilcox—a regular
army captain and a man in his late thirties—was dissatisfied.
He was *only* a brigadier general. Lee, preoccupied as he
might have been by the fact that the Army of the Potomac
was moving against him, nevertheless tried to handle the
personal matter in as considerate a way as possible. He replied to Cadmus:

"I am pained to find you desire to leave the army. I
cannot consent to it for I require your service here. You must
come and see me and tell me what is the matter. I know you
are too good a soldier not to serve where it is necessary for
the benefit of the Confederacy."[8]

Wilcox apparently didn't let Lee alone know of his discontent, for after his transfer request was denied, a petition
signed by two Confederate generals and no fewer than sixteen congressmen was sent to Jefferson Davis advocating
promotion for Wilcox. A few months later, after rendering
outstanding service in the battle at Salem Church, Wilcox
indicated that the desire for advancement was still gnawing
at him when he wrote his sister not of what his victory meant
to the Southern interests, but of its effect on his chances of
promotion:

"If I am not promoted now I shall be really discouraged
for I know that no one could do more than I have done with
the means at my command. Everyone is talking about the
injustice done me and I am now really sick with disgust."[9]

Dorsey Pender, a favorite of Lee's, showed his character
when he revealed his attitude toward advancement in a letter to his wife in North Carolina:

"I shall be promoted some of these days, I do not feel any
uncomfortable uneasiness about the matter . . . I want the
promotion as much for your sake as anything else. I should
like for those who have known of me to know you are the
wife of a general and from supposed merit and not of political
influence."[10]

So indispensable were the professional soldiers with Lee

that few thought of withdrawing from the field no matter how ghastly the wounds they suffered. They took only as much time to heal as was absolutely required and reported themselves back for duty in whatever shape they were in. Dick Ewell, who lost a leg at Groveton, returned nine months later with an ill-fitting artificial limb that gave him constant pain. To ride, he had to be strapped to his horse. Francis Nicholls of Louisiana, class of '55 and late of the 3rd Artillery, suffered the loss of an eye, an arm, and a foot in separate battles before he pronounced himself no longer capable of continuing in the field. Disfigurements went almost unnoticed because they were so commonplace. A wound about the mouth made it almost impossible for General Arnold Elzey of Maryland to speak, but the gruff, hard-drinking 2nd Artillery captain remained in uniform and struggled as best he could to make himself understood.

It was, of course, a different age, one in which such concepts as honor and duty held a higher value and motivated some men to extreme behavior. Who can tell what it was that caused Brigadier General John M. Jones to give up his life so seemingly needlessly in the Battle of the Wilderness? Some 53,000 men would be killed, wounded, or captured in those tangled thickets in a month, nearly 2,000 a day, and Jones's loss was one of the saddest and one of the first.

He was a West Pointer, class of '41, who had taught infantry tactics for seven years at the academy, including the period when Lee was superintendent. They would come into contact again later in Texas and New Mexico when Jones pulled frontier duty, and much to Jones's misfortune.

A man forty-one years old when the war broke out, a full captain in the regular army and with twenty years experience to his credit, in this army Jones commanded not even a regiment at a time when men with a fraction of his service time were becoming brigadiers and major generals. For the first two years of the war he served in such nominal posts as assistant adjutant general and inspector general at the divisional level. Though repeatedly commended for bravery and efficiency, Jones was regularly overlooked by Lee for higher rank.

What was it? Why was Jones being held back, his friends wondered. Promotion finally came after Chancellorsville at a time when the army was beginning to run low on general officer material. Only then did Lee reveal to Jefferson Davis that he was recommending him for promotion on one condition, which was that, should Jones "fail in his duty, he will instantly resign."[11]

His men quickly became attached to Jones—a Virginian with a thick Mark Twain–like mustache and long, thick brown hair—particularly, as has been mentioned, for his efforts to keep them in the best physical condition possible.

There are several versions of how he was slain during the stampede of his command. In one he is said to have died in a desperate effort to rally his brigade; but in another he is pictured as calmly set on his horse gazing at the approaching enemy while his men were flying past him, a man who simply had done all the running he ever intended to do.

Others, in Jones's fashion, did their duty and occupied the place they felt their station demanded no matter what the hazard, but that is not to say they were not relieved when the danger had passed.

Brigadier General Dodson Ramseur, a darkly handsome but prematurely balding infantry commander, had written his young wife when he learned he was to be promoted to major general though only in his mid-twenties:

"I will be the most rejoiced on your account, first, because you will be pleased at the honors conferred on me and, second, because I'll not be so much exposed. If I am a division commander now and stay off further from the line, I'll tell you of my escapes.

"I have had three horses shot under me and disabled, one of these was struck three times. In addition to these, the pony was also slightly wounded in the leg but not disabled. My saddle was shot through the pommel. I got four holes through my overcoat besides the ball that passed through my arm. I tell you these things, my darling wife, in order that you may be still more grateful to our Heavenly Father for his most wonderful and merciful preservation of my life."[12]

Three months later, Ramseur was killed in action.

Despite their common commitment, and the fact that all faced a rather ominous future should their cause fail, the West Pointers with Lee formed something less than a harmonious band.

The causes of friction were varied but the squabbling was incessant; at times so many generals were placed under arrest by their superiors, for charges ranging from "want of confidence" to insubordination, that Lee was hard pressed to find enough officers of equal rank to form the court martial boards to hear the complaints, as regulations required . . . and what sticklers for regulations these men were!

Very often the simple explanation for the trouble was a personality conflict, for rarely has such a collection of diverse manners and natures been assembled. Some difficulties were deep-seated and actually dated back to cadet days. Many believe that the cold, aloof posture Stonewall Jackson assumed with his subordinates after attaining the lofty rank of major general was a response to the smug, superior way in which he himself had been treated by his classmates when he arrived at West Point as a humorless, ungainly plebe. Brigadier General Lewis Armistead of Pickett's Division had been expelled from the academy for losing his temper and breaking a plate in the mess hall over the head of another cadet, Jubal Early, who was now also a general serving with Lee, and there is no indication that either time or their changed status improved their relationship.

In correspondence with their wives and friends, the Confederate leaders did not mince words in describing their feelings toward some of their brother officers. The candid Dorsey Pender had known Jeb Stuart, the flamboyant cavalry leader, for years; when the possibility of Jeb's transfer to the infantry was being considered, Dorsey told his wife, Fanny:

"He is a scheming fellow as ever you saw. I do not like him over much and would not have him command the corps for anything in the world."[13]

He also showed himself to be no great admirer of old Stonewall, saying once that he coveted promotion only as "a means of getting out of Jackson's command."[14]

Lafayette McLaws, the commander of a First Corps division, apparently shared Pender's low opinion of Jeb and complained to a confidant about the *beau sabeur:*

"Stuart carries around with him a banjo player and a special correspondent. This claptrap is noticed and lauded as a pervocity (sic) of genius when in fact it is nothing else but the act of a buffoon to attract attention."[15]

While arrest and court martial was the conventional course for settling difficulties, sometimes another solution was entertained—pistols. Relations between Longstreet and the fiery A. P. Hill once reached the point at which a hostile meeting between the two generals was almost certain and seconds actually had been chosen. Only Lee's personal intervention avoided a confrontation.*

The commanding general's most effective tool for relieving friction was transfer; that is, reassigning the subordinate to another corps or, if no suitable vacancy existed, out of the Army of Northern Virginia. But the process cost Lee too many trained officers he could ill afford to lose.

Jackson, without doubt, had the poorest relations with his subordinates and made flagrant use of the court martial procedure. He would have a junior officer arrested for what seemed the most absurd of reasons, and hostility in his camp was intense.

One not untypical incident involved Jackson and A. P. Hill shortly after the latter had been transferred to the Sec-

---

*In another Confederate army, one West Pointer, Marmaduke, '57, actually had slain another academy man, L. M. Walker, '50, in a duel.

ond Corps because of a squabble with Longstreet. An aide described how, during the Antietam campaign, Hill was riding at the head of his division and observing the usual interval when, on taking a casual look back, he saw that the column had been halted and he was riding off, as it were, on his own.

Turning his mount, he galloped up to the commander of the leading brigade and demanded to know why he had halted without orders. The colonel, placed on the spot, merely pointed to General Jackson, dismounted nearby, and said the corps commander had told him to stop. Hill was off his horse in an instant, striding up to Stonewall; he drew his sword and, presenting the hilt, said, "If you take command of my troops in my presence, take my sword also."

Jackson, rarely disposed to calm down and pacify an angry subordinate, replied coldly, "Put up your sword and consider yourself in arrest."[16]

Hill was made to march at the rear of his command, eating the dust they raised. That day he was wearing an old white hat slouched down over his eyes, his coat was off and he had on an old red flannel shirt and was looking, to one private, "as mad as a bull."[17] However, for once in his life Jackson reconsidered a decision and decided to release Hill just before the battle of Sharpsburg. This was fortunate for the army for it was Powell who would bring his powerful Light Division on the field at the very moment the army appeared ready to collapse, and save the day after an incredible forced march from Harpers Ferry.

Another victim of Jackson's wrath was Brigadier General Richard B. Garnett, a forty-four-year-old professional soldier from a Virginia gentry family who had succeeded him in command of the Stonewall Brigade.

Garnett, whom Jackson might have known in Mexico, had quickly won the affection of his men for his apparent concern for their welfare and needs, solicitation which some thought went a bit too far for a unit needed for hard service.

At Kernstown, during the Valley Campaign in 1862,

Jackson ran into the troops of the Union General Shields and, vastly underestimating their strength, decided to attack. This time it was Jackson who was up against a stonewall. When he was spent, Union counterattacks began battering Garnett's sector. Finally, ammunition began to run out. Garnett did what he thought was the only sensible thing to do: He ordered a withdrawal. When Garnett pulled out, the whole line had to retreat and abandon the field. Jackson was furious and ordered Garnett placed under arrest, fuming that his men should have been ordered to use their bayonets when their cartridges were gone.

Garnett tried for nearly a year to have his case heard but it never came up. Relieved from command, he waited idly in Richmond to be either restored or reassigned. He was there when, after Chancellorsville, the body of Jackson was borne to the capitol for a state funeral. Despite his own difficulties with the man, Garnett was heard to manfully comment to one of the fallen general's aides:

"You know of the unfortunate breach between General Jackson and myself. I can never forget it, nor cease to regret it. But I wish here to assure you that no one can lament his death more sincerely than I do. I believe he did me great injustice but I believe also he acted from the purest motives. He is dead. Who can fill his place?"[18]

Another cause of animosity within the officer corps that caused Lee no little grief was the belief of some that Virginians were being shown favoritism in advancement by the Confederate authorities.

Pender, for example, was convinced he was going to be passed over for major general when command of the Light Division opened up because, as he wrote Fanny, "I have two drawbacks and heavy ones too—I am a North Carolinian and a friend of General Hill. The first will work against me with Mr. Davis and the latter with General Jackson."[19]

Dorsey himself was guilty of the injustice of giving priority to men of his own state, and frankly admitted refusing the

services of a first-rate commissary officer because he was not
a North Carolinian and Dorsey felt there should be more
Tarheels in the army command.

Longstreet showed his belief that state prejudice existed
when he declared that the only thing that prevented Daniel
Harvey Hill or McLaws from being made commander of the
Third Corps, instead of A. P. Hill, when that corps was created was "the objection that they were not Virginians."[20]

Lee often did make a special effort to give his units
officers from their own states, recognizing how much more
closely his troops identified with their states than with the
Confederacy, and knowing their anxiety to maintain as much
autonomy as possible. Nevertheless, the fact that five of his
nine infantry division commanders at the time of the Gettysburg campaign, two of his three infantry corps commanders,
his cavalry leader and his artillery head all were Virginians
did indicate that a degree of geographic imbalance existed in
the high command. It was more apparent when it was considered that only a quarter of the 166 infantry regiments in the
army were from Virginia. North Carolina with thirty-four
infantry regiments and Georgia with thirty-three had not
nearly as many leaders in the army.

But all was not discord, jealousy, and conflict within the
officer corps. Lee did manage to impress on his leaders the
great purpose of their service and, when necessary, reminded them of it. There were many more close relationships among the officers than antagonistic situations. Richmond was, of course, the social center and when officers of
the widely dispersed units got together it was usually at some
event in the crowded Confederate capital city, to which so
many of their wives and families had "refugeed" to escape
the invading Yankees or be closer to Lee's army.

The city, swollen to a population of more than 140,000
compared to less than a third of that in prewar days, was a
study in contradiction. It was a place where a life of culture
and gentility continued to coexist with the brothels and gam-

bling halls that had opened by the score for the soldiers; a society in which ladies and gentlemen of gentry families dressed in their finest to attend balls and parties at homes where the hosts were able to provide only the simplest refreshments for a buffet; a bustling thoroughfare through which a constant, dust-stirring procession of infantrymen and supply wagons passed, dividing the mobs of government workers, excited children, soldiers on leave, and bewildered natives that filled the streets. A visiting Englishman wrote of the scene:

"The idleness and business of war in Richmond are instanced on the one hand by the belted and spurred braggarts who lounge about the hotels, the closed shops, the schools that keep perpetual holiday, the old men that gather in the shady side walks to gossip and bewail and the negro women that scream delightedly at the peals of music. And on the other, by the thousands of workmen that frame oddly-constructed floating batteries at the waterside and forge great guns at the Tredegar works, the medley of transportation teams that rumble over the bridges and file along the turnpike roads, the gangs of negro men that are marched under guard to work at entrenchments and government buildings. War looks at you from hospital churches and through the bright eyes of fever, it thrills you in the limp of cripples that beg at the wayside, it whispers sadly in the rustle of crape, and shouts its discontent in the yells of newsboys."[21]

Hood, commander of the wild Texans, was a familiar figure in the city and was often seen riding in President Davis's carriage. Edward Johnson was very much in the social whirl, his booming voice roaring above all others at the bar of the Spotswood Hotel and shattering the subdued atmosphere of drawing room gatherings of the local aristocracy. A. P. Hill, of an old established family, had countless relatives in the city and was a regular visitor with his wife, the stunningly beautiful Dolly Morgan, sister of the famous Confederate raider, John Hunt Morgan. Harry Heth, Hill's West Point classmate and mischievous chum, and Harry's engaging younger brother and aide, Stockton Heth—whose family had operated mines just outside the city for decades—were figures as popular in the city for their gentlemanliness and good humor as they were at army headquarters. Lee himself had his family installed in a red brick townhouse on Franklin Street, which the ladies had all but converted to a factory turning out clothing and bandages for the army.

Recuperating officers in the city became objects of good-natured solicitation and their wounds, to whatever extent possible, were made laughing matters—Dick Ewell trying awkwardly to adjust to his peg leg, a young lady having to cut Dodson Ramseur's food at table as if he were a child because of his paralyzed arm, the amusing whistling sound a cavalry officer made when he breathed because of a bullet wound in his throat.

Richmond. To the Longstreets, who only a few months after their arrival lost three of their children to an epidemic, it was a place of tragedy, as it was to so many others who followed riderless horses with army boots reversed in the stirrups of the saddles up Main Street to Hollywood Cemetery, or who labored at sprawling Chimborazo Hospital. For the audiences at the Richmond Theatre and Metropolitan Hall, and the splendidly-gowned guests of Varina Davis at the presidential mansion, it was a place of gaiety. For the officers of Lee's army it became, in effect, the Confederacy. It was what they were defending, the society to which they were committed. If it fell to the Union armies, it meant they were done.

5

"A Handful of Lieutenants"

"THERE IS ONE West Pointer, I think in Missouri, little known and where I hope the Northern people will not find out. I mean Sam Grant. I knew him well at the Academy and in Mexico. I should fear him more than any of their officers I have yet heard of. He is not a man of genius but he is clear-headed, quick and daring."[1]

That was the way Dick Ewell analyzed their future adversary for his fellow Confederates in May 1861, and a keen analysis it was, too. Yet the observations also served to vividly show another strange aspect of this war in which these officers were involved. That is, the ability each side had to hastily construct a complete dossier, based on long personal association, of any leader who emerged on the scene. Someone in camp would have known the subject at virtually every stage of his development and would be able to contribute to a characterization of his strengths and limitations.

Such familiarity made it difficult for officers of either side to surprise or confuse the other; they all knew each other's tendencies and capacities too well—who was rash and reckless, who plodding and cautious; which were capable of complex maneuvers, which dull and unimaginative.

Beyond that, another built-in problem of having men

from the same school leading both armies was that they had learned the same lessons from the same teachers. Like two protégés of the same chess master in confrontation, it was difficult for either to make a move that appeared in any way foreign or unorthodox to the opponent.

The mentor of many at the academy had been Dennis Hart Mahan, a short, hot-tempered Irishman with a sharp tongue, who was the senior member of the faculty board. So many of the martial dicta he imbued in the cadets would find manifestation on Civil War battlefields that Mahan's influence was unmistakable.

"Attack the enemy suddenly when he is not prepared to resist," Mahan had emphasized . . . as Stonewall Jackson would do on Hooker's exposed right flank at Chancellorsville, and as Longstreet would against Pope at Second Manassas.[2]

Apply maximum effort against the enemy's weakest point, Mahan had dictated . . . as Longstreet would in exploiting the gap in the Union center at Chickamauga by organizing a formation of eight brigades and advancing in column at half distance, so that each unit could be wheeled either right or left and present a regular line of battle against any force attempting to seal the opening.

"Celerity," Mahan had emphasized. "No great success can be hoped for in war in which rapid movements do not enter as an element" . . . as A. P. Hill would so aptly demonstrate in viciously driving his division from Harpers Ferry in time to save the day at Sharpsburg.[3]

"Secrecy, good troops and a thorough knowledge of the localities are indispensable," Mahan had asserted . . . and no doubt had the ear of Cadet Jackson who displayed the principles with such spectacular success in the Shenandoah.[4]

And Mahan had also stressed the value of information, saying "too often a general has only conjecture to go on and that based on false premises" . . . a point to which Cadet Jeb Stuart must have paid particular attention, for as a cavalry leader he would render his most important service to Lee as an incredible information gatherer.[5]

The Union side also had its West Point graduates (nearly three times as many as joined the Confederacy) who had listened to the same lectures; however, just as among the Southerners, there were those capable of applying the rules and a proportionate share who lacked the intelligence, charisma, or other qualities necessary to effectively use them. Certainly when Mahan was stressing "Assume the initiative" to Cadet John Bell Hood he did not have in mind the type of reckless offensive General John Bell Hood would launch in Tennessee in 1864.

That the Southern leaders from West Point came more quickly to prominence in the war than the West Pointers serving the Union was due in part to the policies of their respective governments in regard to the trained officers. On the Northern side, the high command's approach was to keep these officers with their small regular army units, and only later did they achieve positions of control in their army equal to the influence the Southern graduates exercised.

Beyond assignment policy, it must be remembered in assessing the relative roles of the West Pointers that they inherited two totally different sets of conditions in terms of the materiel support provided by their governments, their comparative freedom to operate, and the manpower with which they had to work.

On the Union side, the deep fervency of its volunteers from the New England towns and Midwest farms was diluted by the indifference of the hordes of new immigrants the government conscripted and the substitutes it permitted to take the places of men wealthy enough to buy their way out of military service.

Among the Southerners, the personnel problems were of a different sort. Here ardor was undermined by the recruit's stubborn refusal to give up his footloose independence and individuality and surrender himself to order, discipline, and conformity. The Confederate officer, generally speaking, was working with rustic young men more familiar with firearms, more accustomed to the outdoors, and more simple and devoted than his opponents, but also a great deal less used to being told what to do. In some ways, the products of the teeming Northern cities, the youths raised in crowded slums, were tougher physically than the Southerners. For one thing, they proved to be far more immune than the country boys to the diseases that were encouraged by congested camps and confined quarters. In short, both classes of recruit had their innate strengths and weaknesses. And both sets seemed equally adept at contracting the "social" diseases, one area in which neither was anxious to gain recognition of superiority.

Perhaps the main difference between the positions of the two groups of officers was that one was serving in an established army augmented with volunteers and the other had to create an army from scratch . . . and with precious little time to do it.

When those 169 delegates to the secession convention gathered in venerable Institute Hall in Charleston and "opened the ball" by bravely proclaiming to the world that "the Union now existing between South Carolina and other states, under the name of 'The United States of America,' is hereby dissolved," it was obvious that little or no thought was given in advance to just what might be required to back those words with a formidable military force if the Federal government was not willing to accept the declaration.

Even Jefferson Davis, a West Pointer who should have realized what was entailed in putting together an army, did not exhibit any appreciation of the magnitude of the problem when he called for 100,000 volunteers to stand ready to meet whatever response might come from Washington to restore the union.

They had managed to forge their army, these Rebels from West Point, and this clearly was their first and perhaps most important contribution. There was nothing very neat or precise about what they had fashioned but that awful, confused crowd of volunteers with which they had started had been organized into some manageable state. A visitor to the camp of a good soldier like Dorsey Pender, that strong, dark-eyed young North Carolinian, could note that they were "a model of cleanliness, regularity and good order; his sentinels and guard saluted in strict military style; all officers wore the badges of their rank."[6]

Badges of rank? Don't think for a moment of brass bars or oak leaf clusters. Pender himself indicated his lofty station with a pair of black stars cut from felt and sewn on the collar of his rough gray tunic. It was just another effort on Dorsey's part to do as well as he could with what he had at hand.

But Pender's unit was by no means the norm for this newly-formed army. There was such disparity between the appearance and behavior of the various brigades in their dress, camping routines, and style of marching that they became recognizable by them. To go to the other end of the spectrum, one could visit the squalid camps of John Bell Hood's division. An inspector general, who did, found that the living conditions of the 1st Texas Regiment around Fredericksburg reflected "inexcusable neglect on the part of its officers."[7] After reading several such reports, Lee concluded that "Hood is a good fighter, very industrious on the battle-field, careless off."[8]

A visiting Coldstream Guards officer who had been favorably impressed with the marching of Lafayette McLaws's division, observing "no attempt to straggling," was almost taken aback by the sight of Hood's men passing through a town:

"This division, well known for its fighting qualities . . . certainly are a queer lot to look at. They carry less than any other troops, many of them have only got an old piece of carpet or rug as baggage, many have discarded their shoes in the mud, all are ragged and dirty but full of good humor and confidence in themselves and in their general, Hood. They answered the numerous taunts of the Chambersburg ladies with cheers and laughter."[9]

After two years in the field, there wasn't a regiment uniformed anything like the Royal Hussars though none looked quite as bad as Hood's tatterdemalions. Most of the soldiers in the army were in patched garb that could be replaced only by stripping the bodies of the dead. A high percentage were barefoot. There was no soap available and the men were physically filthy, reeking of perspiration and waste, their faces carrying black powder smears weeks after each engagement. Hair was long and matted; those who cared about their teeth carried toothbrushes in the button-holes of their lapels but could count on no professional dental attention.

Straggling on the march reached enormous proportions and there were as many fighting men lining the roadsides as the army passed as there were in ranks. The men who dropped out temporarily did so for one of three basic reasons: to bandage or rest their battered feet, to forage for some food, or, most commonly, to relieve their dysentery. It was a condition that most of the officers had come to accept.

Campgrounds were sickening indeed. There were few tents, and men slept on blankets sometimes spread over rub-ber sheets they unfolded on the ground in no particular pat-tern in the general area assigned to their regiment. There were no tools to dig latrines and the odors emanating from any site inhabited for more than a day were overwhelming. The men banded together in messes of five or six to fry globs of dough in a common pan and called it bread, or munched on roasted ears of corn. In truth, no man with any respect for his wife or sister would dare bring her anywhere near where the troops were encamped. But as shabbily cared for as they were by their revolutionary government, the spirit of these men in the ranks remained indomitable and their plain, basic courage admirable. The wonder is that so many stayed with their commands as long as they did.

Most civil leaders in the South were willing to give the West Pointers full credit for their ability to so quickly shape this new army, and for their success in instilling some form of discipline over a class of men not easy to manage. Their unsightly appearance was recognized as a matter of logistical failure and not their leaders' indifference. But when it came to the battlefield, just what was the professional soldiers' influence? It was those spirited, shrieking boys in the ranks who were driving the Yankees from the field. It was they who deserved the credit, not their leaders with their textbook tactics, a good many politicians would obstinately argue. If anything, some felt, the West Pointers inhibited the army's prowess; one of those was the plantation-born South Carolina colonel who wrote smugly:

"When an army is confined for military leaders to a handful of lieutenants who have never seen more than a regiment, probably not more than a company in action, and have never had to deal with a harder problem in the maintenance of their men than how to get a wagon train from the nearest railroad station, it is apt to be hurt by the restriction."[10]

The colonel would have received no argument from Union General Irvin McDowell about the extent of their experience in the "old army." He told a congressional committee, in explaining the shortcomings displayed at Bull Run, that "there was not a man in the whole army who had ever maneuvered troops in large bodies." McDowell said he "had seen them handled abroad in reviews and marches but I had never handled that number and no one here had. I wanted very much a little time, all of us wanted it. We did not have a bit of it."[11]

To what extent they adjusted and managed to contribute to the art of war can be given over to the group of professional soldiers from European armies who came here to observe the conduct of the conflict, to comment on objectively.

Primarily, the foreign observers were interested in weapons and tactics. The troops themselves did not impress them that favorably. To Count Helmuth von Moltke, the great Prussian strategist, it was a war being fought between "two armed mobs."[12] To Sir Garnet Wolseley, creator of the modern British army, the infantrymen looked like "very raw levies" and the horsemen "irregular Indian cavalry."[13] What intrigued them all, however, was the improvisation that was being demonstrated.

It was the first war any of them had ever known in which the railroad was utilized as a means of speedily transporting troops from one sector to another, and they could see how strategy had become geared to the capture or protection of the vital rail lines. These foreigners could also recognize that the introduction of field fortifications by Lee's army after Gettysburg, when it was forced into a defensive posture, might revolutionize infantry warfare even if they could not then identify the practice as a precursor of trench warfare. It was astounding indeed for them to watch the infantrymen felling trees and stripping fences to set up barricades to crouch behind as soon as they were placed in position. In Europe, infantrymen were simply left exposed (and could be driven from their positions much more readily than the Confederates were seen to be dislodged).

But it was the cavalry tactics being introduced by Jeb Stuart, Fitzhugh Lee, and the other Confederate horsemen that most impressed them. And not the spectacular rides around the Union armies the gray squadrons performed—those jaunts were discounted as showy demonstrations that may have helped morale a bit but accomplished little and probably only served to wear down the riders as well as their mounts. It was the concept of cavalry being armed with rifles instead of sabres and using horses merely as a means of transportation to get swiftly to the points where the soldiers were needed to fight on foot. These Americans had recognized that the rifled musket with an accurate range of half a mile had made obsolete both the bayonet and the practice of using cavalry as shock troops against infantry, thundering upon them with slashing swords. Mounted men could get nowhere near an infantry line now without being toppled. But to quickly get an armed brigade of troops to a threatened railroad junction or to a ford to prevent a crossing—this was the new combat role for cavalry the Stuarts had discovered, which completely altered the use of that arm of the military for the rest of its day.

On the strategic level, the Southern leaders were in a position to participate and contribute to a much greater degree than their Northern counterparts who were under almost constant cabinet pressure. Lee, particularly, enjoyed a relationship with his government no Union general until Grant could claim. He had its complete confidence and a great deal of latitude in movement. Far more than the Burnsides or the Popes, he was in a position to control the course of the war. Lee and virtually all his subalterns were inclined toward the offensive. They thought in terms of bold steps that would bring about quick victory. Less than two months after the terrible blood-letting of the Seven Days, Lee was looking for a way to bring pressure on the North and moved his army into Maryland. The next year, weeks after suffering the heaviest casualties to date at Chancellorsville, he was advocating a second invasion to reap the benefits of victory, gain the foreign recognition that might make a difference, and capture Harrisburg or some other major Northern city. Similarly, Jackson had waited on the heights of Fredericksburg with growing impatience for Burnside to exhaust himself. No soft sentimental feelings for Ambrose were entertained by Stonewall. He was straining for the opportunity to counterattack and destroy the Union Army in the field and was thoroughly disheartened—while others rejoiced—to see the blue-clad soldiers recross the river and get away.

Ultimately, the war would be lost in the manner Lee predicted it would be—when the South was no longer able to take the offensive.

In searching for the essence of the part played by the West Pointers from the South in the war, the simple answer may be that it was they who provided the glue that held the Confederate army together and gave it cohesion, order, and a degree of professionalism. Without them there would have been utter chaos. Lee himself acknowledged that the calibre of volunteers who had joined him was "the best in the world" and he was certain they could successfully resist any force that could be brought against them. But only, the commander emphasized, "if properly disciplined and instructed."[14] It was for this that the West Pointers were most needed and on this score alone, if they had contributed nothing else, their place in the history of the Confederacy was firm.

6

"A Desperate Thing to Attempt"

THE GETTYSBURG CAMPAIGN exposed all the weaknesses of the command structure of the Army of Northern Virginia. The heavy casualties sustained in the battle, losses that could not be replaced, emphasized the lack of depth in the officer pool. The confusion, uncertainty, and inaction of several men in key positions revealed they had been advanced too far, too soon. The fact that many failed under pressure there who had already established themselves on other fields gave Lee evidence that two years of combat was beginning to show on the nerves of his lieutenants.

The outcome of that summer campaign of 1863 was a shock to both the high officers of the army as well as the men in the ranks, the trauma intensified by the fact that all had been sure of success when they headed toward Pennsylvania.

"There was not an officer or soldier in the Army of Northern Virginia, from General Lee to the drummer boy, who did not believe . . . that it was able to drive the Federal army into the Atlantic Ocean," wrote one division commander, Harry Heth.[1]

With all the army's self-assurance, its thinking men also realized the vast importance of the expedition. There was a keen sense of now-or-never, a general awareness of the fact that the army might not ever again have an opportunity to take the offensive and wrest a victory in the field. This sense of high purpose was evident in the final letters coming from Lee's army as the movement got under way. The men did not know exactly where they were headed. Baltimore? Harrisburg? It did not matter. They knew they were exercising the initiative; they were advancing and it was toward the Potomac and Yankeedom.

"Keep in good spirits, honey, and hope that this summer's work will help shorten the war," wrote battle-scarred Dorsey Pender to Fanny who was concerned about the moral implications of a Southern army invading the North. The young husband, now commanding a division, was hardly as disturbed as she. If General Lee felt decisive victory could be achieved by taking the offensive, Pender was ready to follow no matter what boundaries were crossed. His parting line to his young wife was simply, "Have no fear that we shall not beat them."[2]

Lee had achieved his greatest victory only weeks before at Chancellorsville and without two of his nine infantry divisions—Pickett's and Hood's—which had been on detached service. His top-ranking officers had performed superbly in the tangled thickets where each was called upon to act virtually independently to resist Hooker's multipronged movement across the Rappahannock. With a force half the size of the Federal commander's, the Rebels had sent the Union Army fleeing in chaos. The flanking movement Jackson had executed would go down in military annals as one of the great tactical strokes of warfare.

Stonewall himself was the main casualty of Chancellorsville, and to compensate for that immeasurable loss, Lee had reorganized his army into three corps instead of two, giving command of Jackson's reduced Second Corps to one of his division commanders—Dick Ewell—and the new Third Corps to A. P. Hill, the hard-hitting Light Division commander. The former had been absent from the army for ten months recuperating from the loss of a leg at Groveton, but both men were highly regarded and no concern was felt over their elevation to corps command.

Although the Chancellorsville losses had been heavy, the arrival of a number of fresh regiments from North Carolina had helped fill the ranks and Lee was nearly at peak strength, in command of a force of about 55,000 infantry, 12,000 cavalry, and 4,000 artillerymen for the invasion.

At no point in the war would he have more major units under the control of West Pointers. All three infantry corps commanders and eight of the nine infantry division commanders were academy graduates. Only Robert E. Rodes, who had won promotion by spearheading Jackson's devastating flank attack against Hooker's right at Chancellorsville, was not of the academy. The thirty-four-year-old railroad engineer was a product of the Virginia Military Institute. Of the thirty-seven infantry brigade commanders, eight were West Pointers, three were former regular army officers who had not graduated from the academy, and five were out of V.M.I. In the cavalry, the commander and three of his five brigadiers were West Point trained.

Before the army withdrew from Gettysburg, however, the infantry alone would have fourteen of its brigade and division commanders killed, wounded, or captured, including seven West Pointers.

Gettysburg, a remote, unfamiliar place to the boys from Mississippi and Georgia in the ranks. But to a large number of Lee's officers the town was quite well known because Carlisle Barracks, the cavalry school, was only thirty miles away and they had pulled tours of duty as instructors there. Ewell and Anderson had served there together in the late forties; Longstreet's first son was born at Carlisle while his father was stationed at the post. Fitzhugh Lee, "Maryland" Steuart, Beverly Robertson, and Dorsey Pender also had been assigned there and Lee himself had once conducted a court martial at Carlisle.

Now, even though they came as invaders, those passing through Carlisle made a point of calling to pay their respects at the homes where they had been received socially, and while their dusty troops lolled about outside the officers in gray "were courteously received and entertained."

First among the West Pointers to fall when the battle began was one of the most popular members of the company, the engaging Virginian Harry Heth (one of the very few generals whom Lee addressed by his first name). Harry was grazed on the side of the head by a minié ball as he was directing his division during the opening clash with the Union First Corps off the Cashtown Road. He would have been a dead man, Heth was convinced, had not a wad of paper he had inserted in the band of a too large beaver hat he had procured in Chambersburg a few days before cushioned the blow. As it was, he was rendered unconscious for more than a day and removed from the sharp criticism being voiced against him. His peers were upset with Harry for, in his first fight as a division commander, violating one of their principles. He had committed the army to a major battle before it had had an opportunity to consolidate and select the ground.

In that same meeting engagement, prompted by Heth's benevolent quest for shoes in the town for his barefoot men, Brigadier General James J. Archer of Tennessee, an old 9th Infantry captain, was captured by a big Irish private of the Iron Brigade. As he was being hurried to the rear, who should be encountered but the Federal General Abner Doubleday, who knew Archer well enough from the old service to call out, "Well, Archer, I'm glad to see you."

The bagged Confederate brigadier retorted sourly, "Well, I'm not glad to see you. Not by a damn sight."[3]

Ewell also met a minié ball that day. An officer who was with the new Second Corps commander when it struck asked quickly, "Are you hurt, sir?"

"No, no," Old Baldy replied lispingly, "I'm not hurt. But

suppose that ball had struck you. We would have had the trouble of carrying you off the field, sir. You see how much better fixed for a fight I am than you are? It don't hurt a bit to be shot in a wooden leg."[4]

The wonder is that there was that much humor left in the harassed corps commander after all he had been through that day.

Then Hood, the forceful leader of the Texas Division, went down with a wound that would paralyze his right arm just as he was leading his crack troops into the attack on Little Round Top and the Devil's Den the next day—an attack he had launched only after a prolonged argument in that friction-filled army of individualists with his corps commander, Longstreet, as to the direction he should take.

Later that same afternoon, as he lounged with his staff near a seemingly protective boulder, waiting for the progressive attack Lee had ordered to involve his division, Dorsey Pender was struck in the leg by a fragment of a stray shell.

The wound was in the soft part of the thigh and bleeding was instantly intense but yet the injury was not thought to be very serious. A bandaged Pender was such a familiar sight to his men there was no particular alarm when they saw him being attended. The battle still was raging when Pender was carried to an ambulance and started back to Virginia. En route, the wounded leg became infected and when the wagon arrived in Staunton, a virtual hospital city, the limb was amputated. The operation was performed too late; gangrene had spread too far and Pender died. He was but twenty-nine years old. His death came in a campaign from which the North Carolinian was drawing no satisfaction despite its early successes. His last letter to Fanny from Pennsylvania mentioned "the people are frightened to death and will do anything we intimate to them . . . I am tired of invasion for although they have made us suffer all that people can suffer I cannot get my resentment to that point to make me feel indifferent to what goes on here."[5] Dorsey would be sorely missed.

West Point in the 1850s. *(Courtesy of United States Military Academy Museum.)*

The proprietor and his legendary establishment; Benny Havens and his tavern by the Hudson River below the cliffs of Highland Falls. *(Courtesy of USMA Archives.)*

Gen. Robert E. Lee served as superintendent of West Point, 1852–55. *(Courtesy of Valentine Museum.)*

President Jefferson Davis, too, was a West Pointer, class of '28. *(Courtesy of Valentine Museum.)*

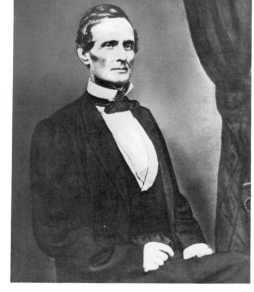

Two West Point roommates and the lady both had wooed— Confederate Lt. Gen. A. P. Hill and Union Maj. Gen. George B. McClellan and his wife, the former Ellen Marcy. *(Courtesy of Valentine Museum) (Courtesy of Virginia State Library.)*

Confederate Lt. Gen. James Longstreet (above) and Union General Ulysses S. Grant—and their wives—had been close friends since the officers served together at Jefferson Barracks in the 1840s. *(Both courtesy of Valentine Museum.)*

The incorrigible West Point pranksters, Confederate Maj. Gen. Henry Heth (left) and Union Maj. Gen. Ambrose Burnside, whose friendship endured long after the Civil War. *(Courtesy of Virginia Historical Society; courtesy of Valentine Museum.)*

Lt. Gen. Thomas J. Jackson, who learned well his lessons in strategy at West Point. *(Courtesy of Virginia State Library.)*

Lt. Gen. Richard S. Ewell, an old dragoon captain, regretted deeply his having to leave the U.S. Army. *(Courtesy of Valentine Museum.)*

Lt. Gen. John B. Hood, whom the brilliant James B. McPherson tutored at West Point. Tragically, McPherson was killed before Hood's lines at Atlanta. *(Courtesy of Valentine Museum.)*

Maj. Gen. Lafayette McLaws, a strict officer the men called "Make Laws." *(Courtesy of Valentine Museum.)*

Maj. Gen. George E. Pickett, the showy leader made famous for his charge at Gettysburg. *(Courtesy of Valentine Museum.)*

Lt. Gen. Jubal Early led the daring raid on Washington in 1864. *(Courtesy of Valentine Museum.)*

Maj. Gen. Edward Johnson found many considerate old friends among his captors at Spotsylvania. *(Courtesy of Valentine Museum.)*

Lt. Gen. Richard H. Anderson was one of thirty-two members of the class of 1842 to become Union or Confederate generals. *(Courtesy of Valentine Museum.)*

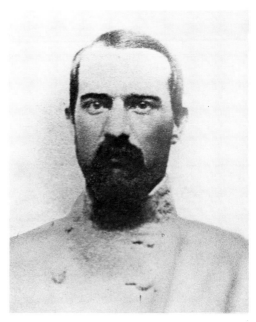

Maj. Gen. W. Dorsey Pender, whose fatal wounding at Gettysburg was a heavy loss to the Confederacy. *(Courtesy of Valentine Museum.)*

Maj. Gen. J. E. B. Stuart, the Rebel cavalry commander whose father-in-law, Philip St. George Cooke, was a Union cavalry leader. *(Courtesy of Valentine Museum.)*

Maj. Gen. Fitzhugh Lee, a favorite, was serenaded by the cadets when he left the academy faculty to go South. *(Courtesy of Valentine Museum.)*

Brig. Gen. William N. Pendleton was an Episcopal minister when the war broke out. *(Courtesy of Virginia State Library.)*

Brig. Gen. E. Porter Alexander directed the cannonade before Pickett's Charge. *(Courtesy of Valentine Museum.)*

Maj. Gen. Stephen Dodson Ramseur was cared for during his last hours by Custer and other Union officers he knew at West Point after he was mortally wounded and captured at Cedar Creek. *(Courtesy of Valentine Museum.)*

Brig. Gen. Junius Daniel was among the outstanding officers killed in the Wilderness. *(Courtesy of Valentine Museum.)*

Brig. Gen. Lewis Armistead, killed at Gettysburg, had been expelled from West Point after a mess hall fracas with Cadet Jubal Early. *(Courtesy of Valentine Museum.)*

Brig. Gen. George Steuart was regarded as a martinet by his men. *(Courtesy of Valentine Museum.)*

Brig. Gen. John M. Jones regained his reputation at the cost of his life in the Wilderness. *(Courtesy of Valentine Museum.)*

Maj. Gen. Cadmus M. Wilcox had four Union generals and four Confederate generals as pallbearers at his funeral. *(Courtesy of Valentine Museum.)*

Brig. Gen. Francis Nicholls suffered the loss of an eye, an arm, and a foot during the war. *(Courtesy of Valentine Museum.)*

Gen. P. G. T. Beauregard served briefly as superintendent of the military academy just before the breakup. *(Courtesy of Valentine Museum.)*

Maj. Gen. Gustavus Smith feigned his own death to make his way South and join the Confederacy. *(Courtesy of Valentine Museum.)*

Gen. Joseph E. Johnston, the skillful commander of the Army of Tennessee. *(Courtesy of Valentine Museum.)*

Maj. Gen. Arnold Elzey, one of the roughened veteran U.S. Army officers who joined the Confederacy. *(Courtesy of Valentine Museum.)*

Brig. Gen. Nathan "Shanks" Evans partied with Union army chums between battles. *(Courtesy of Valentine Museum.)*

Lt. Gen. Daniel Harvey Hill, Jackson's brother-in-law, led by fearless example. *(Courtesy of Valentine Museum.)*

Maj. Gen. Thomas L. Rosser, whom Union General Custer cautioned not to expose himself in combat so recklessly. *(Courtesy of Valentine Museum.)*

The third day at Gettysburg was George E. Pickett's day. If he saw destiny at work in his behalf as he led his division on to the field—the only fresh, unbled body of men Lee had left to spearhead his go-for-broke assault on the Union center—fortune was also making her presence known in a melancholy way to several other of the old army men serving under the showy Virginian.

Pickett's troops, despite efforts to keep them from seeing the large open area over which they would have to advance by restricting them to the other side of the crest of Seminary Ridge, soon found what was required of them and their moods changed abruptly. Said one Virginia colonel, "From being unusually merry and hilarious they on a sudden had become as still and thoughtful as Quakers at a love feast."[6]

An artillery officer, visiting friends in Brigadier General Richard Garnett's brigade, found several officers openly speculating on the chances of getting safely through the attack.

Dick Garnett, finally restored to a command months after being humiliatingly relieved by Jackson at Kernstown, was himself apprehensive. Sick and bundled up in his blue U. S. Army overcoat for warmth though the temperature was in the 90s, Garnett stood next to his long-time friend, Lewis Armistead, and studied the mile of clear pasture his troops must traverse and the far-off Federal position bristling with riflemen. Finally he remarked, "This is a desperate thing to attempt."[7]

There was no doubt that Dick was "going up," though he was ill enough to be in a hospital. To compound his malady, he had suffered the painful indignity of being kicked in the leg by a horse as he passed a wagon column at night and could barely walk. But the shame that Jackson had heaped on the proud Tidewater Virginian had left him with only one burning desire, to restore his honor and his family's name, and he was going to take part in this charge even if he had to be carried.

Whether his body or his spirit needed fortification, Garnett joined Cadmus Wilcox, in his straw hat and short round jacket and more nervous than ever, in the orchard of the Spangler farm where they and some staff officers passed around a captured bottle of Pennsylvania whiskey during the long wait prior to the advance. Between swigs, the officers chewed on some cold mutton that Cadmus provided. And they talked about what was ahead of them. How many glances were taken by the Confederates at that distant ridge bustling with activity? How many soldiers made vows to themselves as did a sergeant of the 14th Tennessee who, seeing what was expected of him, asked himself, "June Kimble are you going to do your duty today?" and firmly replied, "I'll do it, so help me God."[8]

For his part, Pickett appeared to be delighted with his great opportunity, his supreme moment in the war. Thousands of men noticed him riding about, a small blue cap tilted jauntily on the side of his head, his long blond locks streaming beneath it. He paused here and there to give some personal instructions or inquire about this or that. Cheerful and sanguine, he obviously believed himself lucky to have the chance to lead the great assault. Infantryman R. A. Shotwell, in a different mood, one of grim resignation, remembered his general as looking "rather dandyish in his ruffles and curls, well mounted and ready to ride to death if need be."[9]

At 1:30 P.M. Longstreet, opposed to the assault, brooding and sullen, sent a message to his artillery chief: "Let the batteries open."

On signal from a section of the Washington Artillery, the most ear-shattering cannonade ever heard on the continent got under way. Between the Confederate and the Union field pieces, a total of 245 cannons were firing, creating two great clouds of smoke. The attacking troops were by now advanced to the edge of the woods of Seminary Ridge, which paralleled the one they were to assault, and were lying prone against the artillery fire. Someone appealed to rough, gray-haired old Lewis Armistead to take cover as the fire intensified.

"Never mind me, boys. We need men with guns today," the brigadier replied.[10]

The whole affair was particularly painful for Armistead. When the war broke out and he had made his decision to return to Virginia, Armistead's closest friend in the army, Winfield Scott Hancock, it will be recalled, gave him and other returning Southern officers a farewell party at the little adobe post at Los Angeles where they were then stationed. Now, two years later—and three thousand miles removed— here was Armistead's brigade getting prepared to attack the very corps commanded by Hancock on Cemetery Ridge.

Armistead. How tragedy seemed to stalk him. His boy-hood dream ruined when he was expelled from West Point over that mess hall fracas with Jubal Early, he had stayed on in the army anyway. He had made his way slowly up to the rank of captain in the 6th Infantry. Lee had gotten to know him well at Fort Riley, Kansas, and knew something few others did about him. How Armistead had had to leave the fort with his company while an epidemic was running through it. The unit was thirty miles away when it was over-taken by a courier with the news that Mrs. Armistead was dead, succumbing to the disease only six hours after she was taken ill. He had returned in the night, buried his wife in the morning, and started for his camp carrying his two children with him. Said Lee to his own wife at Arlington of the sad incident, "A soldier has a hard life and but little consider-ation."[11]

More orders came from Pickett. A rider told Brigadier James Kemper, commander of the third brigade in the divi-sion, "You and your staff and field officers to go in dis-mounted. Dress on Garnett and take the red barn for your objective point." The rider recalled later that, as he deliv-ered the instructions over the noise of the barrage, Kemper stood up and removed a handkerchief from under his hat, with which he had covered his face to keep the gravel knocked up by the fierce artillery fire from his eyes.[12]

The strain of defenselessly enduring the violent cannonade was enormous on the Confederate riflemen. A Virginia soldier relieved it a trifle for the men around him when, seeing a hare race across the field, he shouted in encouragement, "Run, you lil ol' rabbit. If I was a little ol' rabbit stead of a man I'd run too."[13]

During the firing, Longstreet made a ride along the front of Pickett's men, no doubt to steady them. With little formality, one man called out, "You'll get your old fool head knocked off; we'll fight without your leading us."

But, someone observed, "he was as quiet as an old farmer riding over his plantation on a Sunday morning and looked neither to the right or left."[14]

As he watched the projectiles from the Confederate guns falling over a broad area, most well behind the Union front line on Cemetery Ridge, Brigadier General Henry J. Hunt, chief of artillery of the Army of the Potomac, wore a look of disgust. He had personally trained a good many of the Southern artillery officers before the war and was not at all pleased with their work today. Their fire should have been concentrated on the point of attack. Years later when he encountered General Armistead Long of Lee's staff, a West Pointer, class of '53, who had served under him in the U. S. 1st Artillery, Hunt told him that he was not satisfied with the conduct of this cannonade and that he had not done justice to his instruction. After listening to the criticism, Long replied to his mentor, "I remembered my lessons at the time and, when the fire became so scattered, wondered what you would think about it."[15]

After the shelling had been going on for nearly an hour, artillery leader E. Porter Alexander scribbled a note to Pickett:

"If you are to advance at all, you must come at once or we will not be able to support you as we ought. But the enemy's fire has not slackened materially and there are still 18 guns firing from the cemetery."[16]

Pickett, who in his anxiety had three times inquired of Alexander if it were not yet time to charge, ordered his men in line.

When the assault troops began filtering out of the thicket and forming in the open, regiment after regiment straightening out from loose, confused crowds of ragged figures with arms ferried at all angles, into orderly, motionless lines— silent save for the staccato shouts of the officers shaping them —a spectacular sight was created. At no time before or after would the Union soldiers or even the Confederates, for that matter, have a view of so large a portion of the Army of Northern Virginia. The force of 12,000 infantrymen might not, as Longstreet feared, be large enough to accomplish its mission, but it was the largest wholly visible assemblage of Confederate infantry ever organized and it was an awesome scene. The private waiting in the ranks of the 7th Virginia of Kemper's Brigade on the extreme Confederate right, straining his eyes down the mile-long line of gray and brownish figures, colored at intervals by bright red battle-flags and blue Virginia state banners, to where the 11th Mississippi troops of Brigadier General Joe Davis were forming, must have felt the comfort of numbers to a sublime degree. How could such a tremendous force be repulsed?

If there was any lag in preparations, arrangements instantly were speeded when Alexander rushed another note to Pickett:

"For God's sake, come quick or we cannot support you. Ammunition nearly out."[17]

When Pickett cantered up to his friend Longstreet and said, "I shall lead my division forward, sir," the corps commander, fully convinced there was no hope of success but under Lee's orders, was too depressed to voice a reply. He merely nodded.

Garnett and a few others ignored the order to go in on foot. Dick would never have made it. He mounted a big black horse, a beautiful animal that attracted much attention,

Union and Confederate; and white, weak, and grim, he trotted to his position.

"Up, men, and to your posts," Pickett called out. "Don't forget today that you are from Old Virginia."

Far down the line, the magnificent J. Johnston Pettigrew, commanding Heth's bloodied division that day, sang out, "Now, Colonel, for the honor of the good old North State, forward!"

Turning to the standard-bearer of the 53rd Virginia, General Armistead asked, "Sergeant, are you going to put those colors on the enemy's works today?"

"I will try, sir, and if mortal man can do it, it shall be done!"[18]

Cadmus Wilcox, on his white pony, intercepted Pickett as the troops started forward and offered his flask to his academy classmate.

"Take a drink with me—in an hour you'll be in hell or glory," Cadmus entreated. Pickett declined.[19]

The whole thing was over in even less than an hour. It was more like thirty minutes. There was simply too much open ground to cross; it was too far for that many men to march under solid shot artillery fire, then skirmisher sniping and finally infantry line fire and double canister, and still be capable of doing damage when they finally reached the crest. One statistic indicates what it was like. A board on a fence that Archer's Tennessee brigade had to cross—a plank fourteen inches wide and sixteen feet long—showed 836 holes after the battle.

A riderless black charger, galloping wildly about the field, blood streaming from its face and body, let the army know that Garnett was down.

On the left, canister had taken off the leg of old Isaac Trimble, a West Point–trained railroad builder who had been given Pender's place in the charge.

They had all started off in beautiful order in three distinct lines. First the frightened came running back. Then the wounded returned in growing volume as the charge progressed. No cohesive body ever came back, just a swarm of hurrying men scattered across a vast open field hoping they could somehow make it to their lines without feeling a bullet in their backs.

Armistead had driven his Virginians, about two or three hundred anyway, right in among the guns before he went down. In the end, Lewis was almost a Quixote figure for he had been trying to give direction by waving his hat on the tip of his sword. But the felt was riddled with holes and kept sliding down the blade to the hilt. On Cemetery Ridge, his men probably presented more truly than the 7th Cavalry the type of scene suggested by the Currier & Ives poster of Custer's last stand. A Union soldier who saw the nearly surrounded Confederates making their fight on the ridge in the copse they had taken as their objective wrote:

"The grove was fairly jammed with Pickett's men, in all positions, lying and kneeling. Back from the edge were many standing and firing over those in front. . . . Every foot of ground was occupied by men engaged in mortal combat, who were in every possible position which can be taken while under arms or lying wounded and dead."[20]

Pickett was not one of the men on the crest. He was observing the struggle through his field glasses from the vicinity of the red barn of the Codori farm on the Emmitsburg road, halfway across the field. As division commander, that was as far as he chose to go. When he realized it was all over for his men, he collapsed emotionally. Unnerved, tears streaming down his cheeks, he got on his horse and spurred it toward the Confederate lines.

"Where is General Longstreet?" he was yelling as he galloped by, his long hair waving in the wind. A courier was sent to intercept George and when he was brought to Longstreet the first thing he said was, "General, I am ruined. My division is gone—it is destroyed."[21]

Whether or not he noted the subjective view that George was taking toward the tragedy, "Old Pete" tried to console him and assure him that things would not be as bad as he thought.

Pickett was still crying when he approached an infantry colonel and said, "Why did you not halt my men here? Great God, where, oh where is my division?"

The reply was that George saw around him what was left of it.[22]

Another witness to the division commander's distraught state noted that "General Pickett broke into tears while General Lee rode up and they shook hands." He then turned to the remnant of his command and said, "You can go back to the wagons and rest until you are needed."[23] Then he rode on alone toward the rear. When he composed himself he wrote to his teen-aged fiancée of how other units had failed to give him proper support in the charge and, not very gallantly or honestly, added that it was a miracle that he had escaped unharmed. Neither Pickett nor his division would ever recover from the shattering defeat they had suffered.

The disaster was of awesome proportions. Upon the crest, Union soldiers were collecting thirty-three Confederate battle flags strewn on the ground and marching off thousands of prisoners, men who had given up rather than risk a bullet in the back trying to race back down the slope to their lines.

There was no "I told you so" spirit about Longstreet when the calamity was over. He knew how much his fatherly stability was needed now and he did not spare himself. In fact, he as much as Lee exerted his strength of body and personality to help the troops recover from the shock and prepare to defend themselves against the counterattack the Confederate leaders were certain was coming. Longstreet had observed the charge while sitting atop a rail fence, whittling. When Colonel Fremantle of the Coldstream Guards arrived on the field late, he exclaimed to Longstreet, "General, I wouldn't have missed this for anything."

Longstreet boomed back, "I should very much have liked to miss it; we've attacked and been repulsed."[24]

Before leaving Fremantle to do what he could to repair the damage, Longstreet said to the Britisher that he could use a drink. Did he happen to have anything? Fremantle offered his canteen of rum from which Longstreet took a long pull and then went to work.

Lee was magnificent at that moment. He rode among the retreating soldiers, saying to them "It is all my fault" and appealing to them to help him stave off further disaster.

Wilcox, whose Alabama brigade was thrown in on the right as a reinforcement after all hope of success was passed and was thereby needlessly sacrificed, was in tears when he rode up to Lee.

"General, I have tried to rally my men but as yet they will not stand," he said.

"Never mind, General, the fault is all mine. All that you have to do is help me to remedy it so far as you can."[25]

Up on the fateful ridge, the mortally wounded Armistead called weakly for help "as the son of a widow" and two Yankee soldiers who understood the Masonic code tried to aid him. A Union surgeon led to Armistead found him seriously wounded, completely exhausted, and seemingly broken-spirited.

At one point, Armistead whispered to the physician, "Say to General Hancock for me that I have done him and you all a grievous injury which I shall always regret."[26]

With the message, Hancock received Armistead's watch and side arms. The old veteran died in a Federal field hospital two days later and his body was taken to Baltimore by a friend and buried in St. Paul's Churchyard.

The souvenir hunters made short work of Garnett's body, stripping it so completely of all signs of rank that he was interred in one of the mass graves scooped out on the field and was never individually identified. Years after the war, the tragic soldier's silver sword would be found in a Baltimore pawnshop.

A Confederate of no special prominence summed up the

failure: "We gained nothing but glory and lost our bravest men."[27]

As disturbing as were the losses of key officers in the campaign was the indication that a dreadful mistake may have been made in the advancement of two generals beyond their capacities—Richard Ewell and A. P. Hill.

Both of the new corps commanders seemingly underwent metamorphic changes the first time they faced a combat situation with the responsibility of three divisions each on their shoulders. Ewell became indecisive. When the Union forces had been routed on the first day at Gettysburg and had scampered up the hills beyond the town, the army looked to the always-aggressive dragoon to follow through with his corps and attack Cemetery Hill before the enemy could reorganize. But Ewell could not move himself to give the orders. He hesitated, he questioned, he waited, he reread his discretionary instructions until darkness made his decision for him.

The disappointment in Dick's performance was deepened by the fact that he had made such an exciting initial impression on his troops during the advance up the Shenandoah Valley and into Pennsylvania with his lively spirit and infectious energy.

What had happened to the man at Gettysburg? What had become of the old Ewell? There were at least three things upsetting Dick and hindering his performance. One was the discomfort and misery caused by the ill-fitting artificial leg he had to wear. In order to ride, Dick had to be strapped to his horse by the Apache boy he had brought back with him as a souvenir of his service in the Southwest and kept on as the strangest sort of orderly in the army. When Ewell could not take the torment of riding any longer, he hopped into an open carriage—though he hardly looked martially inspiring when being hauled about in that fashion.

Another factor contributing to the lisping dragoon's growing irritability and agitation as a corps commander was this business of having to interpret Lee's discretionary orders when he was so accustomed to Jackson's specific, optionless instructions. When Lee directed him to do something and then added a phrase like "if practicable," it unsettled Ewell dreadfully. He didn't know what to do, fretted nervously, and diminished himself in the eyes of his subordinates.

The third handicap was Ewell's acquisition, during his convalescence, of a domineering, ambitious wife determined to remake the man in his middle age. Profanity left his speech; church services became part of his Sunday routine. Almost from the day "Mrs. Brown"—as Ewell, for some strange reason, continued to refer to the widow he had married[28]—arrived at Second Corps headquarters after the army returned from Pennsylvania, Ewell's staff was bristling.

"She manages everything from the general's affairs down to the couriers who carry his dispatches," frowned one aide. "All say they are under petticoat government."[29]

Mrs. Ewell did tend to irritate people with her overbearing behavior, a manner developed, no doubt, by having had for years to manage a considerable estate in Tennessee by herself. A smart woman, well educated, she shocked the Confederate officers with her knowledge and opinions of military and political affairs. They were not accustomed to hearing persons of her sex even open their mouths on such subjects.

The degree of resentment the soldiers felt toward the bossy woman and her singularly unattractive daughter who had taken over army headquarters was intense. Said one Marylander rather succinctly, "We were of the opinion that Ewell was not the same soldier he had been when he was a whole man and a single one."[30]

The causes of the change in Ambrose Powell Hill were more mysterious. Lee had once said that after Longstreet and Jackson, "I consider A. P. Hill the best commander with me."[31] Little concern was expressed, when the natty Light Division commander was elevated to corps command, that he would be unable to handle the job. Probably his most pronounced trait was his combativeness. He was a familiar figure on every battlefield, his sword bared; he was usually wearing a red flannel shirt that became known as "Hill's battle shirt." This pugnacious streak is emphasized because at Gettysburg, in his first battle as a corps commander, Hill reported himself too unwell to lead his troops and they had to be taken over by Longstreet. Whatever it was that had incapacitated him, it had come on awfully suddenly because a local resident who had seen him for the first time only the day before distinctly remembered how the Confederate leader seemed "in robust health."[32]

Twice more in the coming months, Hill would suddenly become unavailable in time of crisis because of some malady that was never defined, first in the Battle of the Wilderness and again at Spotsylvania. When he was exercising command, his performance was questionable. At Bristoe Station, he attacked rashly without proper reconnaissance and his troops were slaughtered by Union forces hidden in great rows behind a railroad embankment. After the debacle, Lee toured the field with Powell, heard his explanation, and said tersely, "Well, well, General, bury these poor dead men and let us say no more about it."[33]

After another failure at Jericho Mills, where he had made a piecemeal attack against two Union corps attempting a river crossing, Lee demanded of Hill, "Why did you not do as Jackson would have done, thrown your whole force upon these people and driven them back?"[34]

Hard words for a man of Powell's almost sinful pride to have to hear, more so when his commander was comparing him with a man he so thoroughly despised. One army diarist had to sadly note of the once fiery leader, "A. P. Hill does not sustain himself."[35]

And time would show that neither Ewell nor Hill had suffered but a temporary lapse and were merely having difficulty adjusting to their added responsibilities. No; they were changed men.

7

"Who Could You Put in His Place?"

AFTER THE BLOODIED ARMY had made its tortuous way back from Gettysburg—the combat-dazed soldiers no longer convinced of their invincibility, with so many men missing from the ranks—the West Pointers found themselves with a new, unfamiliar role to fill. Now they must heal.

The stout, square-shouldered figure of Lafayette McLaws, a formidable weight for the little white pony he favored, could be seen regularly about the camps on the Rapidan. Cheeringly, he moved from one cluster of men to another. Are you ready to go at them again, boys? the caped centurion would call out to a group intent on a smoking skillet. We'll soon have things right, boys, he would tell a ring of card players. Usually, the response McLaws got from his men—who had suffered frightfully in the Wheatfield and the Peach Orchard on the second day at Gettysburg—was that they would be ready after a bit, that "we've had all the fighting we want just now."[1]

The solid Georgian was not just putting up a front; his was such an optimistic nature that he could look upon the loss of Vicksburg as a relief.

"The taking of Vicksburg will release our armys,"

McLaws reasoned in a letter to a friend. "We are back again concentrated in the interior and are increasing daily in strength and efficiency. The army has regained all the old spirit and self confidence."

(As for the defeat itself at Gettysburg, McLaws confided to his wife on the way back from Pennsylvania what he was too much of a soldier to ever say in public; that he felt it was Longstreet who had wrecked their chances of the second day:

"I think the attack was unnecessary and the whole plan of battle a very bad one. General Longstreet is to blame for not reconnoitering the ground and for persisting in ordering this assault when his errors were discovered. During this engagement while we were riding [he was] excited giving contradictory orders to every one and was exceedingly overbearing. I consider him a humbug—a man of small capacity, very obstinate, not at all chivalrous, exceedingly conceited and totally selfish. If I can it is my intention to get away from his command. We want Beauregard very much.")[2]

There were many others attempting to minimize the disaster. Colonel Walter Taylor of Lee's staff, who knew the casualty figures, was writing in a similar vein: "This is a grand old army. No despondency here, though we hear of it in Richmond."[3]

How rapidly the men recovered from the trauma of Gettysburg depended in large measure on the consideration and the spirit of their commanding officers. When John Bell Hood saw that his Texans were being put into combat again soon after the battle, he couldn't let them go without him, even though he himself had not healed from the wound he had taken in Pennsylvania. The rangy blond leader was convalescing at a hotel in Richmond when his troops passed the building en route to the train that would take them to Chickamauga. His lifeless arm in a sling, Hood stood on a balcony and parried their rough remarks with a booming voice that carried over their jocular chorus. They wanted Hood with them; they needed him. Sam could not resist. He had his bags packed, gave up the comfort of his Richmond pamperers, and returned to the war long before he should have.[4]

Others were not as conscientious. So badly shattered was George E. Pickett's division at Gettysburg that it had to be pulled out of combat service until it could be reorganized and its depleted ranks refilled. The unit was placed in a quiet sector where George took advantage of the tranquility to marry the Lynchburg Academy student half his age who had so distracted him from his duties earlier in the war. While his division foundered under strange brigadiers and regimental commanders (for only one survived "the charge" unscathed) the newlyweds set up a comfortable nest for themselves in a Petersburg mansion for the winter. As desertion figures in Pickett's division soared to the highest level in the army, a careful Richmond diarist had to sadly record that the perfumed commander was becoming "badly dissipated, it is asserted."[5]

There appeared little prospect, after Gettysburg, of the army ever again becoming strong enough to undertake the strategic offensive. Lee accepted that. What he hoped for was an opportunity, one more chance to score a victory in the field of such proportions that the North would give up in despair the effort to restore the Union.

The battle would be fought on the ground he selected, under the conditions he dictated, not as at Gettysburg where chance had assumed command. The theatre he had chosen for the decisive encounter was that dark, eerie, barely penetrable Wilderness bordering the Rappahannock. Only a few rough, washed-out roads obscured by underbrush snaked through the region, and the passage of the Union troops, artillery, and supply trains over them would be dreadfully slow. It was the ideal place for him to operate, Lee reasoned, an arena where the enemy could not bring its numerical superiority to bear and where the Confederates could break up the advancing army piecemeal.

It was not a totally unfamiliar place, this frightening,

skin-renting thicket in which night often could not be discerned from day. The armies had lost themselves in it during the Chancellorsville campaign and, indeed, there were still bodies in those woods that had never been found for burial. It was not a place to which they wanted to return, a disorienting terrain where a soldier was never sure whether he was facing front or rear, whether the snap of a twig in the tangled scrub meant a scurrying animal or an approaching foe.

When the blue columns started across the Germanna and neighboring fords and began to be swallowed up by the ominous region, word came quickly to Lee from his observation post atop Clark Mountain. His divisions, somewhat restored save for the First Corps units that had been through a winter of bitter fighting in Tennessee, were instantly put in motion to intercept the Union forces and hit them while they were in marching columns and unable to form on the rough ground. Lee was ready for his fight. He was not ready for a Grant.

Taking advantage of obscure back roads and trails known only to local residents, and relying on the alacrity of his infantrymen, Lee was able to detect and exploit gaps in the Union lines as they opened. First in one sector, then another, his howling riflemen would come bursting out of the thickets to send the confused Federals reeling. But the successes were only local. This army was not going to panic as Hooker's had. Reinforcements came up and threatened areas were shored up. And the pressure on the Rebels was reapplied. After each encounter, regardless of what losses they inflicted, it was the Confederates who had to give ground.

It went on for a month. By the time it was over—and places like Spotsylvania and Cold Harbor were returned to nature to disguise and conceal the awful things that had transpired around them—sixteen Confederate generals had been killed, wounded, or captured. Seven of them were West Point professionals. It was a toll more jarring than Gettysburg, one dictated by the nature of the fighting, by combat so savage that no line could have been held without the highest-ranking officers showing a willingness to endure the perils with the men under their orders. One of the earliest blows to the command structure was one of the more grievous, the near-fatal wounding of James Longstreet as he was directing a flank attack that promised to turn the tide at the Battle of the Wilderness.

In incredible similarity to Jackson's experience at Chancellorsville, a Confederate regiment, mistaking the First Corps commander and his staff for Union soldiers in the dense woods, fired a volley that toppled riders one after another. "Dutch" Longstreet was a heavy man with a firm seat in the saddle but the impact of the minié ball that ripped through his shoulder lifted him straight up and he came down hard. Members of his staff rushed to him and managed to get him off his horse and help him to the base of a shade tree. There they found to their alarm that the shot had entered near the throat and the man was almost choking with blood. He needed attention immediately and there was no way of bringing an ambulance to where they were. A litter was found and they started him to the rear. Someone had placed Longstreet's hat over his face to conceal the sight of his heavy bleeding, but he could hear his infantrymen saying that he was dead when their officers were telling them he was only wounded. To reassure them, from time to time, Longstreet raised his hat with his left hand and his pain was eased somewhat by the shouts and cheers the gesture brought from his boys.

Eventually, they got him into an ambulance and took off his hat and coat and boots. The blood had paled out of his face and its somewhat gross aspect was gone. A begrimed man in the ranks who got a glimpse of the corps commander remembered how spotlessly white his socks and his fine gauze undervest were, save where the gore from his wound had stained them. Members of Longstreet's staff surrounded the vehicle, some riding in front, some on one side or the other, one standing on the rear step of the ambulance, seemingly trying to stay as near to him as possible. A man who had been through it all could attest that he "never on any occasion during the four years of the war saw a group of officers and gentlemen more deeply distressed. They were literally bowed down with grief. All of them were in tears. One, by whose side I rode for some distance, was himself severely hurt but he made no allusion to his wound and do not believe he felt it. It was not alone the general they admired who had been shot down—it was, rather, the man they loved."[6]

It was an affection that Jackson never achieved or Lee encouraged. It came not from West Pointers but from a bright, sprightly group of young men who had been bank clerks or university instructors before the war; men whom he had taught, and well, this business of war. The awful truth was that he had become a father to all of them and they could not stand the thought of having to endure this terrifying campaign without his protection.

That wretched wilderness also tore apart a friendship between two Confederate leaders that had been enriched over two decades, the almost brotherly relationship between Powell Hill and Harry Heth. Hill was ill again, secluded in his tent, when Harry, one of his division commanders now, started in on him. Heth's men had been fighting throughout the day and had fallen asleep in exhaustion in whatever place they held when the firing came to a gradual, sporadic end. But it wasn't long before there were disturbing signs of activity among the Federals in front of them, a stirring concealed by darkness and the density of the thicket. Harry, always a little jumpy, more sensitive than ever since his bad experience at Gettysburg, sent word to Hill that he thought he had better arouse the men, replenish ammunition, and construct field fortifications of some sort in the event that a Federal attack was coming. Hill's response was that Harry should relax, that Longstreet's corps would soon be up to relieve him, and that the men needed their rest: Leave them alone.

Lord, what a different fellow Harry was now from that

fun-loving youth so many of his friends remembered! It was
doubtful that he was thinking, on that dark, scary night as he
heard faint sounds of movement in front of him, of that other
night long ago at the academy when he had been straining as
hard to hear the sounds of sentries—the night he led a raid by
ten cadets on the officers' storehouse. The giggling thieves
had made off with a turkey and a keg of wine and congre-
gated in A. P. Hill's quarters to consume it. There, in the
room Powell shared with George McClellan, the group sat
about as silently as possible gnawing on parts of the bird and
passing around a tin dipper, as content as a band of mischievous boys could possibly be.[7]

Once more that night Harry appealed to Powell for permission to awaken his men—though one might have wondered why he felt he needed the authority of his corps commander to take such a step. Once more the weak and
advancingly irritable Hill told him to leave the men be.

Heth and Hill. The good families of Richmond didn't
know of their escapades at West Point, how they had been
the devoted beaus of those two "wild though not bad ladies"
who spent the summer of 1846 in their environs, or of the
haircuts or the turkey raid.[8] They did, however, recall those
newspaper reports a few years later of Harry being killed in
the Indian fighting at Blue Water, and the obituary notices of
him that they had read with dismay. A. P. Hill, crestfallen,
had even joined them in a resolution of sympathy to the
family—only to have Harry reappear safe and sound a day or
two later. The delight of finding out about his own tragic
demise was enough to make his harrowing brush with the
hostiles worthwhile for the playful Heth.

Even in Mexico they had been much together—with
Burnside, of course—though Powell was somewhat preoccupied in those days by the señoritas. "You know my failing," he
admitted. "Tis an inheritance of this family, this partiality for
the women."[9]

No such thoughts tonight. For a third time Heth approached Powell, plunging into his tent to impress on him the urgency of the situation. Hill had had enough.

"Damn it, Heth," he shouted. "I don't want to hear any more about it. The men shall not be disturbed."[10]

Harry whirled around and, friendship aside, went in search of Lee but was unable to find him. It was barely dawn when the Federal attack began, not a crashing onslaught but just a steady, methodical advance by division upon division of bluecoats who had spent their night forming instead of sleeping. The scattered, disorganized Rebels, startled from their slumber, scampered pell-mell to the rear.

So dire was the crisis created by the breakthrough that Lee himself rode in among the panic-stricken men of Heth's and Wilcox's divisions and implored them to stop and make a stand. Disaster was averted when the Texas Brigade and some other First Corps troops arrived and successfully counterattacked to re-store the line. When things calmed down, Heth presented his case to Lee who had a deep affection for him and had personally sought his services. The commanding general's judgment was, "A division commander should always have his division prepared to receive an attack."[11]

The admonition, coming after the criticism of his work at Gettysburg and again at Bristoe Station, hurt Harry deeply. He had not been accustomed to censure. Despite his pranks, he had something of a reputation in the old service as an expert on the rifle and its use by infantry. His book *A System of Target Practice*, was the official range guide used in the army. The change in attitude toward him was making him quite a serious individual. He was no longer that cheerful fellow everyone enjoyed being around.

The fighting attained a peak of fury in the sector that became known as the Bloody Angle, a salient of hastily stacked tree trunks and limbs with a deep ditch in front of it that protruded from the line at Spottsylvania, where the Union troops again broke through. It was in "Allegheny" Ed

Johnson's area of responsibility and he was up there with his men, swinging his huge club wildly in the desperate effort to restore the new breach.

On either side of the line the carnage was awful. A Union officer recalled that "rank after rank was riddled by shot and shell and bayonet thrusts and finally sank, a mass of torn and mutilated corpses. . . . Trees over a foot and a half in diameter were cut completely in two by the incessant musketry fire. . . . We had not only shot down an army, but also a forest. . . . Skulls were crushed with clubbed muskets and men were stabbed to death with swords and bayonets thrust between the logs of the parapets which separated the combatants. . . . Even the darkness failed to stop the fierce contest and the deadly strife did not cease till after midnight."

When he saw the sector the next day, the officer wrote that the dead "were piled upon each other in some places four layers deep. . . . Below the mass of fast-decaying corpses, the convulsive twitching of limbs and the writhing of bodies showed that there were wounded men still alive and struggling to extricate themselves from their horrid entombment."[12]

On the Confederate side, General John B. Gordon, a strikingly handsome Georgian who had been badly disfigured by a minié ball in the cheek at Sharpsburg, gave another perspective to the fighting that went on for more than twenty consecutive hours:

"Firing into one another's faces, beating one another down with clubbed muskets, the front ranks fought across the embankments crest almost within arm's reach, the men behind passing up to them freshly loaded rifles as their own were emptied. As those in front fell, others quickly sprang forward to take their places. On both sides, the dead were piled in heaps. As Confederates fell their bodies rolled into the ditch, and upon their bleeding forms their comrades stood, beating back Grant's furiously charging columns. The coming of the darkness failed to check the raging battle. It only served to increase the awful terror of the scene."[13]

Johnson was only one of several Southern generals and colonels captured in the struggle as they took their places up on the line with the privates and lieutenants in recognition of the seriousness of the situation. A Federal colonel who had an opportunity to observe the high-ranking prisoners while they were being processed noted:

"They have a slight reserve and an absence of all flippancy, on the whole an earnestness of manner which is very becoming to them. They get this, I think, partly from the great hardships they suffer or, still more, the hardships of those at home . . . and from a sense of their ruin if their cause fails."[14]

The bloody Wilderness campaign proved to be too much of a strain on Ewell and he all but fell apart. One officer saw the Second Corps commander as an almost tragicomic character during one day's combat. The old dragoon was standing before a portable field table with writing material on it, his staff a short distance away. Shells were falling fast and furious all about. Every time one exploded near him, Ewell would hop on his good leg and curse with the vehemence of an old trooper and the unction of a new church member.[15]

Soon after the campaign ended, Lee reluctantly had to relieve Dick from command.

"I think his health and nervous system have been shaken by his great injury and, though active and attentive, that he cannot without breaking himself down undergo the arduous duties of corps command," the commanding general advised President Davis.[16]

Ewell was given responsibility for the Richmond defenses but he knew what was being done and it hurt him deeply.

"My position here is without troops," he wrote dejectedly to a friend, "merely a polite way of being laid on the shelf."[17]

With the wounding of Longstreet, the collapse of Ewell, and the illness of Hill, right in the midst of the spring campaign of 1864, Lee found himself with not one of his regular infantry corps commanders on duty. As dire as the command situation had suddenly become, Lee still was not braced for the dispatch that came to him from a place called Yellow Tavern in that same disastrous month of May. Jeb Stuart had been mortally wounded. It seemed utterly unthinkable. There must be a mistake. Others might fall but certainly this spirit could not be stilled.

When Grant had moved across Germanna Ford into the Wilderness, the Union Army's new cavalry commander, Philip H. Sheridan, had lit off on a sweeping raid toward Richmond. Stuart started in pursuit but with little hope of catching the Federal horsemen with his raw-boned, worn-out mounts. It was no longer 1862; the Rebels had run out of forage in war-ravaged Virginia and there were few replacement mounts coming to the army now. Stuart's men could still do vigilant scouting duty, but with horses that chewed the bark off trees for sustenance they were not up to chasing around the countryside after Federal raiders.

When Jeb got to Beaver Dam Station, the Federals had already been there and the supply unit assigned to that place had been forced to burn a million rations of meat lest they fall into Grant's hands. Jeb drove his 5,000 troopers on in weary pursuit. Finally, within sight of the spires of Richmond, Stuart managed to get in front of the Federal riders and set up a line at (for want of a better coordinate to give the battle a name) a ramshackle inn the locals had taken to calling Yellow Tavern. There, dismounted, the gray-coated cavalrymen waited. As the indefatigable Stuart was riding his line with a few of his staff, three Michigan cavalry regiments under George Armstrong Custer attacked and the Wolverines crashed through at a gallop, surging right past Stuart and his aides. Soon the blue riders came dashing back after encountering heavy Rebel fire. Stuart had his pistol out and was peppering the withdrawing Federals and calling to his men as they struggled to expel the attackers from their lines, "Steady men, steady; give it to them."

Almost unnoticed, Private John A. Huff of Company E, 5th Michigan Cavalry, came trotting by. He had lost his horse and he was just trying to get to the rear. He paused only for an instant, to fire a single shot at almost point-blank range at the shouting Confederate officer with the plumed hat. Must be some big bug, he was sure. The bullet struck Jeb in the side and he reeled off balance.

Private Huff slipped away as all attention focused on the wounded cavalry commander. In less than three weeks, Private Huff would be shot dead in a fight at Haw's Shop but he had already done more than his share to bring about the downfall of the Confederacy.

"Are you wounded badly?" the first man to Jeb's side implored.

"I am afraid I am but don't worry, boys," he answered painfully. "Fitz (Fitzhugh Lee, the commanding general's nephew) will do as well for you as I have done."[18]

As they carried him to the rear, Stuart saw some of his disorganized men retreating and the sight seemed to pain him more than his wound.

"Go back, go back and do your duty, as I have done mine," he called out. "I had rather die than be whipped."[19]

Stuart was taken to the home of his brother-in-law, Dr. Charles Brewer on Grace Street in Richmond, where he lingered for nearly twenty-four hours in intense pain. The bullet from the cavalryman's Colt had torn through his abdomen and penetrated the liver and there was no hope for him. The leading figures in the Confederate capital came to his bedside as word spread rapidly that the gallant cavalry leader was badly wounded and had been brought to the city. President Davis was among those who called.

Jeb, only thirty-one years old, spent his last hours putting his affairs in order and, for a man who so loved horses, disposing of his mounts was a matter of extreme importance. He wanted to give them to two of his aides but, to decide which one should have which horse, he asked Major McClellan, "Which is the heavier rider?"

McClellan thought Colonel Venable to be.

"Then let Venable take the gray horse and you take the bay," the general decided.[20]

A lady from Columbia, South Carolina, had sent him a Confederate flag to carry in battle and he wanted it returned. A woman of Shepherdstown, Virginia, was bequeathed his spurs. The cheerful commander, who loved to join in a song, died as a knot of attendants about him sang "Rock of Ages, Cleft For Me."

When Lee was notified of Stuart's loss, he was visibly shaken. The first thought that occurred to him about Stuart was, "He never brought me a piece of false information!"[21]

All that Lee could do to replenish the losses of so many key officers was to advance his most promising division commanders to temporary command of his corps. But their places, in turn, would have to be taken by some inexperienced brigadiers and so the quality of leadership rapidly was diluted. He voiced his despair in a conversation with one of the West Pointers who had been complaining about the failure of a certain politician-turned-general to carry out an attack:

"These men are not an army, they are citizens defending their country. General Wright is not a soldier; he's a lawyer. I cannot do many things that I could do with a trained army. The soldiers know their duties better than the general officers do and they have fought magnificently. Sometimes I would like to mask troops and then deploy them, but if I were to give the proper orders, the general officers would not understand them. So I have to make the best of what I have and lose much time in making dispositions. You understand all this, but if you humiliated General Wright the people of Georgia would not understand.

"Besides," he added, touching on his all-consuming problem now, "who could you put in his place?"[22]

8

"My Bad Old Man"

JUBAL EARLY, "OLD JUBILEE," was a man to be either despised or respected. No one could like him and he seemed determined to make certain no one even made the attempt.

This nasty, bitter, tobacco-spitting, middle-aged bachelor whose rheumatism had made him look almost grotesque possessed one of the best military minds in the South; he might well have been the one leading the Second Corps into Pennsylvania—in Ewell's place—had he been just a trifle more agreeable in personality.

It was the way Early spoke as much as what he said that made him so grating on the nerves of his associates. His voice was described as "a piping treble"[1] and he talked with a long-drawn whine or drawl. To add to it, the man was "startlingly profane."[2]

Henry Kyd Douglas of Jackson's staff found him "arbitrary, cynical with strong prejudice, personally disagreeable," a man who acquired few admirers or friends either by his manners or his habits.[3]

Moxley Sorrel, Longstreet's aide, although seldom within miles of Douglas and the Second Corps, had the same observations, regarding Early as a "snarling, rasping" person whose "irritable disposition and biting tongue made him anything but popular."[4]

Yet, notwithstanding his total lack of personal charm, Early had credentials as a military leader. It was no doubt Jube's record in the field that General Lee was considering exclusively when in the summer of 1864 he chose him to lead the Second Corps—after Ewell was relieved—on a special mission up through the Shenandoah Valley once more. There were two objectives. The immediate one was to stop the Federal General David Hunter, who was putting vast sections to the torch; and the second was to threaten Washington, in the hope that Grant would be forced to send troops there from the Army of the Potomac and thus lessen the pressure on Lee's exhausted troops.

Old Jube too was out of West Point, class of '37, though he had not remained long in uniform. After seeing service against the Seminoles in Florida, Early resigned in 1838 and then studied law in Rocky Mount, Virginia. He later became a member of the House of Delegates and a commonwealth attorney. When the Mexican War broke out, he returned to the army as a major of the First Virginia Volunteers. In Mexico he contracted the rheumatism that was to give him so much trouble throughout his life. Strongly opposed to secession, Early nevertheless went into Confederate service when Virginia left the Union.

He led the 24th Virginia Regiment at First Manassas and, as a brigadier, had a major role in the battle of Williamsburg until a severe shoulder wound forced him off the field. He went on to render outstanding service at Chancellorsville and Antietam. He was called upon to spell both Ewell and A. P. Hill in corps command when they were ill or injured.

While noting his personality flaws, if they could be reduced to that word, Douglas also observed that Early had a mind clear, direct, and comprehensive, and that his opinion was always received with respect by the commanding general who sometimes spoke of him as "my bad old man."[5]

After Jackson, Sorrel thought, none of Lee's subordinates possessed the essential qualities of a military commander to a greater extent than Early. His primary weakness was in his tactics. He just seemed to lack the ability to handle troops effectively in the field.

Not only was his own perception of situations faulty, but he also tended to receive with impatience (and never acted upon) any advice or suggestions his subordinates dared to offer. His distrust of the accuracy of reports he received from scouts, particularly, was well known.

It was also apparent that Early was a man who liked to drink. How much he consumed depended on whether the information was being relayed by one of his supporters or one of his many enemies. A lieutenant in the 12th North Carolina said flatly that the men believed Early was addicted to alcohol, and there were camp stories that he kept a wagon at headquarters that transported only his servant and a keg of brandy. A Savannah News correspondent's report that Early had ridden onto one battlefield with a bottle in his hand, and used it frequently, led to a call for a congressional investigation of his conduct. Early, of course, vehemently denied the charge, claiming his black binoculars may have been mistaken for a jug, and another newspaperman supported him by writing that the stories of his excessive drinking were malicious lies.

Early's own appraisal of Early is one of the more interesting. "I was never blessed with popular or captivating manners and the consequence was that I was often misjudged and thought to be haughty and disdainful in my temperament," he wrote in self-analysis. "I can say, however, that those who knew me best, liked me best."[6]

He seemed more hurt by criticism of his sartorial failings than of his personality and made a point of replying to "some writer who certainly never put himself in a position to see me during the war who had described my dress as being habitually like that of a stage driver. During the war, I was almost constantly in the camp or field except when wounded and I had no time to get new clothes if I had been able. My tastes would always have induced me to dress neatly and genteelly if I could have indulged them."[7]

Jube's standard attire, as has been indicated, included a large white felt hat ornamented by a dark feather, and an immense white though sullied overcoat that extended to his heels.

The corps Early would command in his first major independent mission was hardly recognizable as the same one Ewell had directed at Gettysburg only a year before. The losses of the Wilderness had whittled it down to barely 9,000 men. With "Allegheny" Johnson captured and Early promoted, the division commanders were now Robert Rodes, the V.M.I. engineer now established as one of the top combat leaders in the army; the battle-scarred John B. Gordon; and Dodson Ramseur, the only West Pointer in the trio and at twenty-six the youngest major general in the infantry. There were few familiar names left among the brigadiers. The casualties of the Wilderness had been replaced by unknown colonels with little formal training for command, or bright staff officers whom the leaders they had served deemed more likely to succeed as brigadiers than the senior officers in the units deprived of commanders. The enlisted men were in abominable condition, worn out physically and spiritually after a month of the heaviest fighting the army had seen, and far more ragged than they had ever been.

Morale was not good. After looking over Gordon's division, an amalgamation of a number of shattered brigades, an inspector had to report:

"The discipline in this command is lax. It will be remembered that York's brigade is comprised of the discordant fragments of Hays' and Stafford's brigade and that Terry's is made up of the remnants of the Stonewall, Jones' and Steuart's brigades, formerly of Johnson's division, comprising the remains of 14 regiments. Both officers and men bitterly object to their consolidation into one brigade. Strange officers command strange troops and the difficulties of fusing this incongruous mass are enhanced by constant marching and frequent engagements."[8]

But these were the commanders and the units Jube would have to work with. Personally incapable of stirring and inspiring the troops with either his presence or his oratory, Early simply started off on his grand ruse with a wave and a growl. Moving from Hanover Junction, Early marched his ragamuffin force to Charlottesville where the men boarded trains to Lynchburg, arriving in time to check Hunter advancing in that direction and send him rushing back up the Valley.

"No buttermilk rangers after you now, damn you," Jube snarled as he pursued the Federals.[9] The sarcastic allusion was to the Confederate irregular cavalry that the Union troops had been dealing with exclusively until the Second Corps arrived.

Early chased Hunter to Botetourt Springs and then left him and turned up the Valley pike and trotted his little army of tatterdemalions at Jacksonian speed toward the Potomac. Audaciously, he crossed into Maryland and moved to Frederick, unmistakably headed for Washington. At Monocacy Creek, Jubal encountered and routed a Union force under General Lew Wallace, the general who deservedly was to win more recognition for his writing than his soldiering. In a matter of days, the daring Early was at the outskirts of the nation's capital confronting the outer line of fortifications and the Union Ninth Corps was being rushed by Grant to the city's reinforcement.

Jube never attacked. As he explained, "During the night a dispatch was received from General Bradley Johnson from near Baltimore that two corps had arrived from General Grant's army and that his whole army was probably in motion. As soon as it was light enough to see, I rode to the front and found the parapets lined with troops. I had therefore reluctantly to give up all hopes of capturing Washington after

I had arrived in sight of the dome of the Capitol and given the Federal authorities a terrible fright."[10]

There was little disappointment among the Johnny Rebs over the cancellation of the attack plan. After viewing the massive fortifications there, one staff officer noted that "it was undoubtedly prudent to withdraw and I think it showed good management to come off so well."[11]

As a matter of fact, everything Early had done so far showed good management. He had directed a masterful campaign, succeeding far beyond Lee's expectations and clearly showing his superiority over his predecessor, Ewell, in daring and resolution. But soon the tide turned. Just as Dick Ewell had revealed his weaknesses after first making an impressive debut in the Valley, so apparently were Early's faults to come belatedly to light.

The first setback was due to a mistake by Ramseur. The former 4th Artillery lieutenant had taken his diminutive division out alone to intercept what he thought was a body of cavalry approaching Martinsburg but which turned out to be —after Dodson was isolated and committed—a strong force of infantry. Ramseur's men were sent flying. The younger leader's rashness and carelessness hurt Jubal severely.

"It is sad to think of that mistake which cost us at least 100 men killed and 200 wounded," a gunner of Colonel William Nelson's artillery battalion reflected. "I would not like to be a general having men killed by my errors and mistakes."[12]

For two months more, under constant pressure, Early continued to operate in the Valley—even making another sortie into Maryland—without suffering serious harm. But matters were changing on the Union side. Sheridan had superseded Hunter and was accumulating an army of 50,000 men. When he struck at Winchester in September it was at a time when Early had foolishly split up his small corps again and Ramseur had to face the onslaught alone for hours until the Confederates were reassembled. The day ended with the

Rebels being driven from the field with heavy losses, including that of the brilliant Robert Rodes.

Early's men retreated pell-mell through Winchester and, it seemed, no threat or entreaty could halt them. Mrs. Gordon, the general's lovely young wife who had left their two children with relatives back in Georgia to be with her husband, had tagged along on this campaign, and could be seen flailing about in the dusty street, pathetically trying to stop the fleeing mob. She actually grappled with several of the rough soldiers with her tiny frame and ordered them, with as firm a voice as she could affect, to stop and make a stand. "But neither her example, her rank, nor her beauty stayed them and they trotted on," a staff officer lamented.[13]

At Fisher's Hill, a bluff overlooking Cedar Creek, Early got his corps together once more to face Sheridan but the disaster here was worse, costing him more than 1,500 casualties and fifteen pieces of artillery. Further up the valley, Jubal withdrew, harassed continuously by Sheridan's crack cavalry units. When the Union horsemen had stampeded the jaded, poorly mounted Confederate "Laurel Brigade," Early—who hated cavalrymen—sneered: "The laurel is a running vine."[14]

Lee, hearing of Early's now desperate situation, reinforced him with a First Corps division and some more artillery, and Jube was able to check Sheridan at Waynesboro and force him back. Sheridan then dispersed his force into bands of arsonists to put the valley to the torch, leveling more than 2,700 barns and mills to keep his vow that even a crow flying over the Shenandoah Valley would have to carry its own rations.

Jube pressed his infantry after Sheridan's main force and caught up with it at Cedar Creek. He launched a surprise attack and for a while had the Federals panicked. Unfortunately, so hard up were the Rebels for supplies that when they chased the Yankees out of their camps, thousands stopped to scrounge about for provisions and the attack disintegrated. When the Federals recovered and counterattacked, Early suffered another bad beating, losing a third of his men and thirty pieces of artillery.

Probably no incident of the war demonstrated more touchingly the inseparability of the military academy men than the tragic death of Ramseur.

A short, erect man, Ramseur was extremely handsome with alert dark eyes, despite the premature balding that made him look a decade older than he was. He had been wounded often but the only visible injury was a paralyzed arm that had been hanging limp at his side since the fighting of the Seven Days. He had been married after Gettysburg to Miss Ellen Richmond of Milton, North Carolina, who was very close to delivering her first child when Ramseur wrote to her from New Market:

"I can't help feeling the most intense anxiety and solicitude on your behalf—since our disaster in the Valley my prospect for a furlough is greatly diminished. I think my duty is plain. I ought not to leave now even if I could do so—so my beloved—you must be brave and cheerful without me for a while—to be separated from you is the hardest trial of my life. . . ."[15]

Dodson's last letter was written near Strasburg, two days before his death: "My own darling wife, I received late last night through the Signal Corps the telegram. It has relieved me of the greatest anxiety of my life. I hope that my darling precious wife and my darling babe too are well. . . . I cannot express my feelings. . . . I do not know how I can bear the separation from you much longer. . . . I must see you and be with you and our little darling. The telegram did not state whether we have a son or a daughter.

"Tell Sister Mary for pity's sake if not for love's sake to write me a long letter about my little wife and baby! May God bless my darlings and me and soon reunite us in happiness and peace—a joyful family. Goodbye, sweetheart, with love inexpressible. Your devoted husband."[16]

His face beaming, Ramseur rode out on the battlefield at

Cedar Creek. Encountering Henry Kyd Douglas, the staff officer, he called out, "Douglas, I want to win this battle for I must see my wife and baby."[17]

When the tide turned and his line wavered, Dodson was among his men desperately trying to keep them from bolting when he was shot through both lungs. Adorning his blood-soaked uniform was a little white flower he had put in a lapel to celebrate the birth of his first child, a boy or a girl he would never know.

That night, while Ramseur was being removed from the field in an ambulance, the Union cavalry charged the broken and fleeing remnants of his division.

General George Armstrong Custer, a West Point classmate of Ramseur's, was with the blue troopers and nearby when one cavalryman seized the horses of the ambulance and asked the driver who was inside.

In a weak, husky voice, Ramseur called out in the darkness:

"Do not tell him."

Custer thought he recognized the sound of his old friend and exclaimed: "Is that you, Ramseur?"

When he climbed into the ambulance, "Autie," as the cadets had called Custer, could see how desperately wounded Dodson was and immediately ordered him taken to Sheridan's headquarters where other old academy classmates, including General Wesley Merritt of Illinois and Colonel Alexander C. Pennington of New Jersey, gathered around Ramseur's bed and showed him every tenderness to the last.[18]

The scene was Belle Grove, a plantation near Meadow Mills. A team of Union and Confederate doctors labored together in vain over the young general. In his last hours, to relieve the intense pain, Ramseur was given an anesthetic and he died in a state of unconsciousness. His body was sent through the lines and returned to Lincolnton, North Carolina, for burial. His emotionally shattered wife later received in an envelope a lock of Dodson's hair that George Custer had clipped for her.

It was just one more gesture, one more sign to remind others involved that it was a different war for the academy men and that the conflict reserved a special measure of sadness and anguish for them alone.

The game was up for Old Jubilee.

Early himself referred to the rout of his troops at Cedar Creek as "thorough and disgraceful, mortifying beyond measure. We had within our grasp a great and glorious victory and lost it by the uncontrollable propensity of our men for plunder."[19]

"It was the saddest sight I ever witnessed in the army, to see the utter disorganization of Early's command," a cavalry officer wrote of the scene that night. "Under the cold flickering moonlight I saw regiments pass by and with not over a dozen men in them. The famous Stonewall Brigade was commanded by a captain, and did not number over fifty men. This sad condition of things resulted from a lack of confidence among officers and men in Early as a commander. Why General Lee ever kept him in command was a mystery to everybody."[20]

Lee could go no further with Jubal. In relieving him of the Second Corps, he wrote to Early:

"While my own confidence in your ability, zeal and devotion to the cause is unimpaired, I have nevertheless felt that I could not oppose what seemed to be the current opinion without injustice to your reputation and injury to the service."[21]

Early was left in charge of the Valley district but with virtually no troops. Henry Kyd Douglas, who met him during the last winter of the war when he was passing through Staunton, took the occasion to go to services with the irascible general and soon found his manner had not altered. In the pulpit the preacher, speaking of the dead of the centuries, asked his congregation, for dramatic effect, what they would do if the long departed filed back to earth in some endless procession.

No doubt thinking of the Confederate Army's thinning ranks and the enemy's overwhelming numerical advantage, Jubal responded semi-audibly:

"I'd conscript every damned one of them."[22]

9

"The Gallant Hood of Texas"

THE HAZARDS IN the manner that General Lee was forced to seek out and assign officers to the higher ranks in his army were manifest. The risk involved in taking an "old army" lieutenant, who likely had never seen more than a company of infantry formed in line at one time, and making him a colonel in charge of a regiment was extreme. When the same man, probably in his early thirties, appeared to be capable enough, fit to command the respect of his troops and seemingly able to keep his head when in battle, was then promoted to brigadier general only months later and placed in charge of four regiments, the odds on his success were extended. A year later, when the heavy casualties in the officer corps had to be replaced, the brigadier might then be called on to head a division made up of four brigades, a total of 6,000 to 7,000 infantrymen.

Some men grew with every challenge, including many who had not particularly shone in the old service. Others could extend themselves only so far—their intellect, their training, their experience and, most important, their self-confidence would sustain them through only so many of these rapid and progressively more demanding advancements.

Lee had no choice but to rush his formally trained professionals to the very brink of their capabilities; the posts had to be filled. But it was often tragic when good men who had performed well at lower grades and borne up well through several increases in responsibility were pressed to do more, to assume more authority than they were capable of handling. Witness the experience of such fine soldiers as A. P. Hill and Richard Ewell who had no business in command of 20,000-man infantry corps but had to do as well as they could in the roles assigned them.

No less distressing than the instances of men pushed too far was the effect of the rapid promotion system on men of high ambition, men who for too long had been suppressed in the old army. These were the men who sensed the great opportunity for recognition that was available to those who had only to make themselves conspicuous. Promotion quickly followed nearly every demonstration of skill. The pity was that the gold stars, the public adulation, the power of command over large bodies of troops came too suddenly upon these men who had craved them for so long. They often could not handle them with the assurance of genuine right. It went to their heads. They coveted more attention. They deluded themselves into believing it was not dire necessity that had caused Lee to advance them so quickly, but their own Napoleonic talent alone that had gotten them where they were. Such a case was that of John Bell Hood, a classic victim both of this system that forced men beyond their abilities and of his own boundless ambition.

Though he was only in his early thirties during the war years, few men in the army had been as closely associated with the commanding general—in a geographic sense—as Hood. He had come into the army from duty in Texas where he had served under Lee for several years with the elite 2nd Cavalry, and he had also been to the Point during the period Lee was superintendent. As a matter of fact, it was Lee who had deprived him of a cadet lieutenancy for being absent from quarters. Hood was one of the regulars at Benny Havens and had to thank the tutoring of the brilliant James B. McPherson for enabling him to make up for the study time he squandered, swilling at the legendary cadets' hideaway down by the Hudson. The aid that McPherson unselfishly provided would come to mind sadly years later at Atlanta, when Hood learned that his own men had shot and killed his academy roommate from Ohio.

A measure of Hood's own scholastic ability can be gleaned from the letter he wrote the adjutant general in accepting his commission:

"I received your letter enclosing me a certificate of appointment to the position of Bvt 2nd Lieut U S Army, my age is twenty two years, residence Mount Sterling, Kentucky, appointed a cadet July 1st 1849 & born in the State of Kentucky & hereby accept the appointment of the President and have the oath prescribed by law & enclose you the certificate."[1]

When Hood first came to Virginia with his Texans at the beginning of the war, a South Carolina colonel thought he looked like a raw backwoodsman, gangling, in an ill-fitting uniform with little of the soldierly appearance that West Point often gave its graduates.

Mrs. Chestnut, the Richmond socialite who followed Hood's career in battle and ballroom and would remain his friend at the end when he had few others, noted her own first impression of him in her diary:

"When Hood came with his sad Quixote face, the face of an old Crusader who believed in his cause, his cross and his crown, we were not prepared for such a man as a beaux ideal of the wild Texans."[2]

From the start, his men were ardently attached to him, primarily because he did not try to play the martinet with them, to curb their footloose spirit and attempt to transform them into a palace guard. He was tough but informal, demanding in battle but inclined to turn his back on whatever they did in camp.

As a private named Polley put it, "West Pointer that

Hood was, he not only knew Texas and Arkansas tastes and temperaments but was not unwilling they should be occasionally indulged."[3]

Once when the Texans decided to go AWOL virtually en masse while passing through Richmond, Hood called to one of his officers who was trying frantically to prevent the disintegration of the command:

"Let 'em go, general, let 'em go. They deserve a little indulgence and you'll get them back in time for the next battle."[4]

The Texans showed in the field how much they appreciated the kind of handling they were getting and quickly established themselves as the toughest, most spirited fighters in the army.

Even Pender, the extremely state-conscious North Carolinian, had to admit Hood "has the best material on the continent without a doubt" and that he could strive only to make his brigade "second to none by Hood's Texas boys."[5]

No matter how fierce the fighting, Hood always went into the thick of it with his men. One soldier described Hood as "the coolest man I ever knew. Under all circumstances, no matter how sudden or unexpected an attack might be, he was such a thoroughly-trained soldier that he never showed the least bit of nervous excitement when under fire."[6]

It was after Gaines Mill, where his men had come up against the very company in which Hood had served in Texas, and where they had pierced the center of the Union line, that "Sam" (as his friends called him) began receiving attention in Richmond. At first he was seen mainly in the poker parlors, where he added to the reputation he had gained in Texas as a man who played recklessly and for high stakes. Then he began infiltrating the more genteel society in the capital, maneuvering unabashedly from Mrs. Chesnut's level to the drawing room of the Confederate White House.

Sorrel observed that Hood had very winning manners and "was said to have used these advantages actively for his own advancement,"[7] but Mrs. Chesnut, who was deeply fond of the unpolished war hero, thought his maneuverings anything but subtle.

"General Hood's an awful flatterer—I mean an awkward flatterer," she wrote. Once she told him to his face (after Hood had patronized Jefferson Davis to the point of suggesting the President take the field in active command of the Confederate armies) that "if you stay here in Richmond much longer you will grow to be a courtier. And you came a rough Texan."[8]

But Hood persisted in capitalizing socially on his battlefield achievements, and attaining in society the highest awards he could garner for his services. After every campaign he returned to the social whirl, often being made to look foolish by persons more clever and graceful than he, but nevertheless more and more deeply entrenching himself. Another Richmond chronicler, describing a gala, pointed out how "the blond head of Hood towered over the throng of leading editors, senior wranglers from both houses of Congress and dancing men wasting their time in the vain effort to talk."[9]

Mrs. Chesnut reported hearing at another affair someone smugly remarking: "People who knew General Hood before the war said there was nothing to him. As for losing his property by the war, some say he never had any and that West Point is a pauper's school after all. He has only military glory and that he has gained since the war began."

"Now only military glory!" Burton Harrison, President Davis's secretary, exclaimed in reply. "I like that! The glory and the fame he has gained during the war—that is Hood. What was Napoleon before Toulon? Hood has the impressive dignity of an Indian chief. He has always a little court around him of devoted friends. [Texas Senator Louis T.] Wigfall himself has said he could get within Hood's lines."[10]

In time, Hood began extending his taste for the good life into his field service. While even the commanding general made do with a canvas tent, it was noted at Fredericksburg that Hood had moved into a house and was living in style.[11]

He always had such comforts as fine china and silver at his headquarters, including a silver cup the ladies of Richmond had given him.

The wound Hood received on the second day at Gettysburg was very serious. The arm did not need to be amputated, as initially feared, but practically all feeling was lost and the limb was useless to him the rest of his life. He returned to Virginia in the same ambulance with Wade Hampton, the aristocratic cavalry leader who had been cut on the head with a saber, and gave himself up to the ministrations of the four or five Richmond belles he was reportedly courting simultaneously.

While he was being cared for, a staff officer noted with regret, Hood "suffered himself to criticize very freely our operations in Pennsylvania."[12] How impressive his military expostulations were to the Confederate hierarchy is difficult to say but when Sam went back to the army only a few weeks later for the Chickamauga campaign, it was as a corps commander.

His debut was spectacular as he joined with Longstreet in tearing open with tremendous attacks the gap that some blunder had left in the Union center. Richmond was ecstatic over the success at Chickamauga but was shocked into silence when it was learned that Hood again had been struck down. He had been hit high in the leg by a minié ball. Five inches of bone were fractured and the leg had to be amputated close to the hip. The first reports were that the Texans' commander had been killed and when Lee heard this, he mourned, "I am gradually losing my best men—Jackson, Pender . . . Hood."[13]

After suffering his second dreadful wound in two months, Hood was removed on a stretcher some fifteen miles to the home of Colonel Little where he would spend a month recovering from the amputation. His aide, Henry Percy Brewster, advised Hood's friends in Richmond that the general was in fine spirits and bore it admirably.

About this time Hood was offered a civil post but declined, asserting, "No bombproof place for me; I propose to see this fought out in the field."[14]

He returned to Richmond where he saw a good deal of Mrs. Chesnut and his old group. The bachelor's romantic attention had focused on Sally "Buck" Preston but he apparently made little impression on her as a prospective husband. He particularly annoyed her when, in a fit of temper, he turned on his Negro servant, Cy, for being clumsy in assisting him from a carriage.

"I hate a man who speaks roughly to those who dare not resent it," the young lady made it known. At another point Miss Preston confided to Mrs. Chesnut, rather mysteriously, that now that Hood was going with "those people" she wouldn't marry him "if he had a thousand legs, instead of having just lost one."[15]

When Hood arrived on crutches at a reception held by President Davis with General Preston at his side, tenderly navigating him through the crowd, the crippled general got a thundering ovation. Though pleased at the greeting accorded him, Mrs. Chesnut had to note how demoralizing it was to see a troop commander "so helpless."[16]

Little of the next stage of Hood's career, as a lieutenant general and corps commander under General Joe Johnston, who had succeeded Bragg in command of the Army of Tennessee, stirs admiration for the man. While he did show remarkable grit in returning to the war when so badly hurt physically, he compromised this by taking on the role of unofficial informer to President Davis; he gave the Chief Executive, whom he knew extremely well by now, a running criticism of Johnston's every move, ridiculing his caution and retreats. Eventually the Confederate President took the step that Hood was leading him to but still, when he did, it came as an unbelievable jolt to every man in the army, including Hood himself. The move, of course, was the replacement of Johnston by his disloyal lieutenant.

The change came after General Braxton Bragg, reassigned to duty in Richmond, had been sent as a presidential emissary to assess whether or not Johnston was going to stop his retreating and take the offensive against General William T. Sherman, now at the gates of Atlanta. Bragg didn't tell Johnston why he was there; he led him to believe he was just passing through on a general field inspection of Confederate forces.

Bragg reported to the President that offensive action was the army's only hope and that Johnston was not about to undertake it. "If any change is made, General Hood would give unlimited satisfaction," Bragg opined, adding significantly, "Do not understand me as proposing him (Hood) as a man of genius, or a great general, but as far better in the present emergency than anyone we have available."[17]

Lee had been asked by Davis what he thought of such a change and even he, who had known Sam since he was a teen-aged plebe, could only say, "Hood is a bold fighter. I am doubtful as to other qualities necessary."[18]

The announcement of the change cast the army into utter despair.

"I saw thousands of men cry like babies," wrote Private Sam R. Watkins. He termed the replacement of Johnston with Hood "the most terrible and disastrous blow that the South ever received."[19]

The anti administration Richmond Whig editorialized:

"Hardee is surely entitled both by seniority and by greater experience to the promotion. When and where has Hood displayed the capacity to command one of the largest armies of the Confederacy and to conduct a campaign on which the salvation of the cause to a great measure depends?"[20]

Behind the Union lines, Sherman met with McPherson and John M. Schofield, another classmate of Hood, to assess the change and they concluded they would have to be "unusually cautious and prepared at all times for sallies and for hard fighting because Hood, though not deemed much of a scholar, or of great mental capacity, was undoubtedly a brave, determined and rash man."[21]

The New York *Times* told its readers of this new commander bluntly, that "his whole character is one of utter recklessness."[22]

When told of the move, Hood himself appeared to panic for, in company with two of his generals, he almost immediately telegraphed Davis a request to postpone the change:

"The enemy being now in our common front and making as we suppose a general advance, we deem it dangerous to change commanders, now especially, as this would necessitate other important changes. A few days will probably decide the fate of Atlanta when the campaign may be expected to close for a time allowing a new commander opportunity to get his army in hand and make the necessary changes."[23]

Davis declined to suspend the order. Hood must command.

The impression the mutilated Hood made on the battered Army of Tennessee, devoted to Johnston, was hardly favorable. A thoughtful private wrote:

"I remember when passing by Hood how feeble and decrepit he looked with an arm in a sling and a crutch in the other hand, trying to guide and control his horse. I prayed in my heart that day for General Hood. Poor fellow!"[24]

Hood fought the army the only way he knew how—offensively. His losses were fearful and gained nothing for the Confederacy. At Atlanta, at Nashville, at Franklin he decimated his brigades in one hopeless assault after another against strong positions, always deluding himself into thinking his demoralized, untrusting army was made up of spirited, confident troops like those of his old Texas Brigade. He did not have the same material. This army was beaten the day he took over. As he himself later lamented, the Army of Tennessee "had been so long habituated to security behind breastworks that they had become wedded to the 'timid defensive' policy and naturally regarded with distrust a commander likely to initiate offensive operations."

Finally, at Nashville, Hood had his army shattered by

General George Thomas, the only army on either side to be destroyed in the field during the war. It was the Union's most complete victory, the South's most crushing defeat.

After Nashville, Private Watkins, trudging along with what was left of his unit, passed Hood's field tent and saw him inside.

"He was much agitated and affected, pulling his hair with one hand and crying as though his heart would break while rain drummed a threnody on the roof of his tent."[25]

The crestfallen private, plodding through the mud, remembered how the civilians "seemed to shrink and hide from us as we approached them."[26]

At some point, the men began signing a grim parody to the "Yellow Rose of Texas" that went:

"And now I'm going southward,
    for my heart is full of woe,
"I'm going back to Georgia,
    to find my Uncle Joe,
"You may sing about your dearest maid and sing
    of Rosalie,
"But the gallant Hood of Texas, played hell
    in Tennessee."

Hood did the only thing left for him to do. He asked to be relieved. He returned to Richmond once more but found that the city that had once hailed him as a god now barred its doors to him.

Senator Wigfall, no friend of Hood, said, "Mr. Davis' favor was no less fatal to is object than his animosities. That young man had a fine career before him until Davis undertook to make him what the good Lord had not done—to make a great general of him. He had thus ruined Hood and destroyed the last hope of the Southern Confederacy."[27]

Mrs. Chesnut, of course, still opened her home to Sam though she hardly recognized him when he first appeared, deep in combat fatigue.

"His is a face that speaks of wakeful nights and nerves strung to their utmost tension by anxiety," she told her diary.

"How plainly he spoke out dreadful words about 'my defeat and my discomfiture, my army destroyed, my losses,' etc. He said he had nobody to blame but himself."

After a bit, she had left the room with the general's friend and aide, who had accompanied Hood, and heard him say of his shattered commander:

"He did not hear a word. He has forgotten us all. Did you notice how he stared in the fire? And the lurid spots which came out in his face and the drops of perspiration that stood on his forehead? Yes, he is going over some battle scene; he sees Willie Preston with his heart shot away, he sees the panic at Nashville and the dead on the battlefield at Franklin. That agony on his face comes again and again. I can't keep him out of these absent fits."[28]

But there was not much time to mourn Hood. His personal tragedy was only part of a greater tragedy unfolding more swiftly now, and those who felt sorrow for him could not dwell on it. There were newer and more heartrending appeals being made for their sympathy.

10

"The Marks
of Hard Service"

LEE HIMSELF HAD WARNED: "We must destroy this army of Grant's before he gets to James River. If he gets there, it will become a siege, and then it will be a mere question of time."[1] The Confederate commander had tried vainly to maintain mobility and strike the Army of the Potomac while it was on the move, first at one point and then another in the Wilderness, but despite the losses inflicted, Grant kept sidling to his left, moving stubbornly and inexorably toward Richmond. Lee could only give ground and reposition himself to stay in front of his adversary until there was no more ground to relinquish. Finally, he had to move his exhausted troops into the thirty-six-mile labyrinth of trenches that constituted the Richmond and Petersburg defense line. He was, indeed, under siege.

It was when the army became trapped in the elaborate earthenworks that had so much the mien of a vast open grave that Lee's officers began to discuss openly the likelihood of defeat and its possible consequences. Defeat was one thing for the volunteer soldiers in the ranks, but for the regular army men who had gone in with the Confederacy it was something more dire. And especially if those army regulations dealing with officers who deserted and took up arms for the enemy were to be applied.

There already had been indications that the old army officers were being considered the ringleaders of the rebellion and would be brought to account when the war ended. Those who had fallen into the hands of the Yankees, after initial courtesies from former comrades in blue, now were encountering harsh treatment once out of the combat zone. The experience of James Archer, the "old army" captain who had been taken prisoner at Gettysburg, only served to heighten the concern of the regulars. Once so delicately handsome he had been nicknamed "Polly" by his friends, Archer came back after nearly a year under close confinement at Fort Delaware in shocking condition. Said one Richmond lady who knew him, "There is no trace of feminine beauty about this grim soldier now. He has a hard face, sallow with the saddest eyes. His manners are quiet. He is distracted, weary-looking in mind and body, deadened by long imprisonment."[2] His mother and sister had tried to visit Archer while he was a prisoner but all they were permitted after their arduous journey was a few words with the general while being forced to stand thirty feet away. He tried gamely to return to active service after his exchange and fill one of the vacant command positions but had not the strength. He succumbed only a few months after his release.

Their fate no doubt occupied a good deal of the conversation when the Southern officers came in from the trenches at night and gathered around the tables of the Bollingbrooke Hotel and other shell-damaged meeting places in Petersburg.

Drinking helped many endure the drudgery of the siege and there was apparently a good deal of it. On one occasion an officer came to the door of a log cabin near the lines where, in fact, a prayer meeting was taking place, and beckoned vigorously to a brother officer he recognized passing by to come in and join the group.

"No, I thank you, I've just had a drink" was the shouted

reply he got to his invitation.[3] It was one of the amusing incidents of a period that produced very little to chuckle about. The soldiers spent their entire days in the horrid trenches with no shelter from the summer sun other than that created by rigging a blanket as a roof. To add to their misery, the region was in drought and the parched soil swirled about in choking clouds of dust. The only embellishment to the ditches, cut at all sorts of jagged angles to offer cross fires and prevent the Yanks from bringing power to bear at any single point, was the sharply spiked abatis at their edges. To intensify the overpowering sense of confinement, Union sharpshooters were set up in hundreds of little, bulletproof, basketlike nests in front of the Confederate lines and any Rebel who showed his head for a moment was a dead man.

General Archibald Gracie, about to leave on furlough, was standing on the parapets taking a glimpse through a telescope of the Union lines when he was struck and killed by a fragment of shell. Few of his men had had time to learn much about the stout yet handsome, thirty-two-year-old brigadier who had come to Lee's army late in the war. Most were unaware of the fact that he had actually been born in New York City (of Southern parents) and was appointed to West Point from the state of New Jersey, or that he had studied abroad for several years, at Heidelberg, even before going up the Hudson to the military academy. Gracie had been an Indian fighter of some experience with the U. S. 5th Infantry when he left the service before the war to become a cotton broker in Mobile. He had done well at Chickamauga and was deemed major general timber when he was suddenly lost. His name is preserved today in two odd connections. The first is because his family home in Manhattan, Gracie Mansion, has become the familiar official residence of the city's mayors; and the second is because his son, Archibald Gracie III, also a West Pointer, had the misfortune to book passage on the Titanic. He survived the experience only

long enough to compose one of the most vivid and authorita-
tive reports on the disaster.

Occasionally, the Confederates at Petersburg—spaced
one man to every five yards—were pulled out of their sectors
and moved unnoticed through the interconnected maze to
meet some Union thrust in another locale. Usually the threat
was directed at one of the four broken-down railroads that
supplied not only Petersburg and the army but Richmond as
well. But these respites from the boredom, the imprisonment, the heat, and the body-filth stench of the trenches
were rare.

Henry Kyd Douglas, now transferred from staff to line
duty, recalled the mood at the time:

"Petersburg was virtually surrounded. Daily the inevitable was staring us closer in the face, but we never let on. We
held the lines, slept little, ate less, and at night went about
the town calling and making visits with incredible gaiety. We
were waiting for something to explode, killing time, for time
was killing us."[4]

Some troops entering the trenches for the first time
were aghast at the state of the men occupying them.

"We thought we had before seen men with the marks of
hard service upon them, but the appearance of this division
of Mahone's made us realize for the first time what our comrades in the hottest Petersburg lines were undergoing," one
veteran wrote.

"We were shocked at the condition, the complexion, the
expression of the men . . . even the field officers; indeed we
could scarcely realize that the unwashed, uncombed, unfed
and almost unclad creatures were officers of rank and reputation in the army."[5]

While its handsome brick and white-pillared homes
were pock-marked by siege guns and here and there a win-
dow or a door was out, Petersburg had not been abandoned
and a society of a most unusual sort continued to function.
Mrs. Gordon, in advanced pregnancy, was still with the

army, living in the besieged city. A. P. Hill had his wife, Dolly
—who was mourning the death of her brother, the raider
John Hunt Morgan—installed in a cottage next to Third
Corps headquarters in the plantation house Indiana on the
city's outskirts. Harry Heth's wife was with him also and
Harry came in for some chiding from the commanding general for having become so domesticated he was not paying as
much attention as he should to the state of his fortifications.

The younger blades were not dwelling on the somber
aspect of their situation and with amazing energy, after a
miserable day in the trenches, would gallop into town and
have a dance in progress as soon as a fiddler or piano could be
located. As Douglas, a favorite at such affairs, put it:

"Tenure of life was so uncertain, entertainments,
dances, marriages were plentiful. The sound of parlor music
and of 'dancers dancing in time' might be heard within can-
non shot of the enemy. To go into a parlor for a call or for a
waltz with sword and spurs, while orderlies outside held
horses ready to mount on the first alarm, was no unusual
thing. To spend half the night in the saddle that the other half
might be spent in social revelry was not strange enough to
cause comment."[6]

An artillery officer would recall attending one ball that
not only attracted the misses of Petersburg but a number of
young ladies from Richmond. While it was going on, two
twelve-pounder shells fell in the little front yard of the house,
bursting and throwing dirt over guests who were in the garden, but only stopping the dance for perhaps five minutes.

It was also time for prayer and, in their desperation, the
entreaties of the men took on a grim humor at times. Wrote
General Gordon:

"A deep religious spirit pervaded our army and the
wrestling at the Throne of Grace were of a fervid nature. But
the most devout man could not have helped smiling at some
of the petitions. A tall, gaunt, brave but uneducated man
knelt at my side and in a loud voice said: 'O Lord, we ask for
thy help and favor. We have had some pretty smart fighting,

as thou are probably aware. We beseech that thou will take a proper view of the matter and give us a victory.' But Heaven did not take the view desired."[7]

In October 1864, in fact, on the day Early was fighting the battle of Cedar Creek up in the Valley, Longstreet returned. "Old Pete" was back, the word went through the trenches. His tremendously strong constitution had enabled him to recover more quickly from his near-fatal wounds than the surgeons had thought possible, though his right arm was paralyzed and useless. Following the advice of his doctors, it was noticed, he was forever pulling and rubbing the disabled arm to bring back its life and action. To the boys suffering through the ceaseless siege, Longstreet's return was immeasurably reassuring and Lee was greatly relieved to have him back, particularly because, with the lines so extended, it gave him a trustworthy lieutenant to represent him in far-off sectors he could not regularly supervise personally. And Longstreet did not fail him. Said Fitzhugh Lee:

"At the last . . . he showed still the bulldog tenacity, the old genuine sang-froid which made all feel he could be depended upon to hold fast to his position as long as there was ground to stand upon."[8]

A. P. Hill made some good fights during the long campaign—turning back strong Union thrusts at Globe Tavern, at Ream's Station, and again at Burgess's Mill—and, all in all, became with experience a far more competent corps commander than he had been. But unfortunately his health deteriorated rapidly. Anyone who might have suspected that his incapacitation at Gettysburg and in the Wilderness was psychosomatic could now tell at but a glance that Powell had become a very ill person. What disease it was is uncertain but Hill was wasting away; his cheeks were hollow, his eyes deeply sunken, and his strength gone. A man once most fond of striking attire, Hill now appeared plainly dressed, almost roughly. His genial, friendly personality had altered. A youth who joined the army at Petersburg and met him there for the first time found that "General Hill gave the impression of being reticent or, at any rate, incommunicative. Neither in aspect nor in manner of speech did he appear to measure up to his great fighting record."[9]

But just as Longstreet, Powell Hill had been with the army from the beginning and was determined to be around when the game was up. He was hardly an inspiration to the men, but Powell had a right to a high place on the final muster roll. He had made his contributions—in the Seven Days, at Sharpsburg, and on the railroad embankment at Second Manassas.

Another familiar figure who had rejoined the army on the Petersburg line was Pickett. He of the fragrant curls had been away from Lee almost since Gettysburg, serving in command of the relatively inactive Department of North Carolina, and was returning amidst some furor. Early in 1864, he had conducted a campaign aimed at wresting New Bern from the Federals. It had not gone well. General Robert Hoke was with him and the inability of the two to coordinate their movements had prevented an effective attack. Finally, the effort had had to be written off. But something happened down there in Carolina, an incident about which the principals preferred not to speak for few references are made to it in the memoirs of those involved. No mention whatever is made of the affair by Mrs. LaSalle Pickett in her voluminous writings about her husband. Yet it was an action that very nearly landed George Pickett in the dock as a war criminal at a Nuremberg-like trial.

While his force was in the vicinity of Kinston, a bunch of prisoners, a woebegone set of rustics identified as members of the 2nd North Carolina Volunteers, U.S.A., was brought before Pickett. The men were mainly small farmers of the heavily pro-Union Kinston area. Discovered among them were at least twenty-two men who had formerly belonged to a local "home guard" company. These men had quit the unit when it was incorporated into a regular Confederate Army regiment bound for service in Virginia.

Pickett flew into a rage when the captives were brought before him and he saw North Carolinians garbed in Union blue. He roared at the prisoners, "God damn you! I reckon you'll hardly go back there again, you damned rascals. I'll have you shot and all the other damned rascals who desert."[10]

The irate commander wasted little time in setting up a court martial. In a matter of days, the prisoners who had served in the local unit were found guilty of desertion and sentenced not to be shot but hanged in accordance with the military code covering deserters who take up arms for the enemy. Pickett—he himself a regular U.S. Army captain who had taken up arms against the government—quickly approved the sentences.

While the shocked townspeople of Kinston watched helplessly, Pickett's provost guard constructed gallows near the local jail where the prisoners were crammed together and fed little more than crackers and water while they awaited execution.

Men who had stoically endured war in all its ugliness and fury now had to observe it in a different face, one more revolting than any to which they had been exposed. Men who had had the raw courage to cross that open field at Gettysburg with Garnett and Armistead and Kemper now found themselves struggling within themselves to do nothing but stand in their places and observe the systematic execution of group after group of North Carolinians. No sooner was one trio cut down and carried off than the nooses were applied around another, while their families and neighbors cowered in horror.

A captain of the 8th Georgia Cavalry, who witnessed more than he would ever forget, affirmed, "Sherman had correctly said that war is hell and it really looked it with all those men being hung and shot, as if hell had broke loose in North Carolina."[11]

Another veteran reduced it to but a few words. He said simply, "The sight was an awful one to behold."[12]

So concerned were the officers of Pickett's division at the public response to what was being done by them in Kinston that a colonel of the line issued orders to his combat troops that when off duty they were to go nowhere near the town.

Equally enraged were the Union commanders who had guaranteed the North Carolina enlistees complete protection from the Confederates should they be captured. In the protest sent through the lines to Pickett, some officer unwittingly provided the Rebel commander with the names of other North Carolinians in his custody about whose welfare the Federals were concerned. Pickett acknowledged the roster by sarcastically extending his thanks for the lists "you have so kindly furnished me; and which will enable me to bring to justice many who have up to this time escaped their just deserts."[13]

Estimates of the number of men executed in the little town ran as high as seventy but when Federal authorities put together their case against Pickett he was charged officially with "the unlawful hanging of 22 citizens of North Carolina."[14]

Now the man to whom Lee had said at Gettysburg, "You and your division have covered yourself with glory today,"[15] was back with his commander. The Kinston incident aside, George had rendered one noteworthy service while in independent command. That was in successfully "bottling up" General Benjamin Butler's vastly superior force at Bermuda Hundred and preventing the Federals from grabbing Petersburg while Lee was still in the Wilderness. For this bit of work, Pickett was repaid by Butler's having George's ancestral home on Turkey Island, behind the Union lines in the very section being contested, burned to the ground.

Who knows how deeply Pickett felt this cut? George was not one to suffer long for lack of physical comfort. A young volunteer who joined the army in the war's last year thought Pickett conspicuous at that time for being such "a high and free liver." He said he often heard the showy general declare that "to fight like a gentleman a man must eat and drink like a gentleman."[16] Ironically, Pickett's taste for good food would, before the contest ended, cost the army heavily.

When the armies were stalemated before Petersburg and it appeared the siege would go on for another year, an old army chum of Longstreet's, a Union general named Edward Ord, decided the business had gone on long enough. The politicians were getting nowhere in resolving the issues and bringing about a peace conference. He would take a different approach: Get the old West Point crowd together and just have them agree to end the firing and then let the civil element work out the terms. He actually called "Dutch" out between the lines for a parley under some pretext. And while they stood there—Ord, the Twenty-fourth Corps commander wincing from the pain of the wounds he had taken at Hatchie and Fort Harrison, and Longstreet trying obstinately to rub life back into his deadened arm—the scheme was laid out.

Let's just suspend the fighting, give Grant and Lee a chance to get together and talk, they agreed. And then Ed suggested: Mrs. Longstreet and Mrs. Grant, they're friends since girlhood. Have them get together, and why not have some of the fellows from the academy go along with Mrs. Longstreet into the Union lines?

It was absurd. But their frustration with the seemingly endless war was at such a point that these men were ready to consider any approach that might bring an end to things. The relationship between these officers, and between their wives, was unique in warfare. Longstreet, after all, had introduced Grant to his cousin, Julia Dent, had been present at their wedding and had tried to help him when he was down and out. He was willing to give it a try. He conveyed the plan to Lee, and to Richmond. Considering the South's fortunes at the time, it was decided to go along with the proposal and see what developed. Mrs. Longstreet, who had not seen Mrs. Grant since Jefferson Barracks days, was in Lynchburg when she was ordered to the front by her husband. Understandably bewildered, she nevertheless obeyed and was en route to the capital when Grant got wind of the scheme. It is not difficult to guess where his sympathies rested but he soon put a stop to the plan. In a brief message passed between the lines, he reminded General Lee that such negotiations must be left to the civil arm of the government. Mrs. Longstreet retreated and, lethargically, the siege resumed.[17]

Ewell also was being seen again on the lines. After being relieved of Second Corps command he had been placed in charge of the Richmond defenses, a task—since the army's withdrawal—now shared with Longstreet's corps which was occupying the outer lines while Ewell held the inner defenses. Rounding up troops and materials for his work under the rowdy, chaotic conditions that now existed in the capital was exasperating work, hardly suitable for a man of Ewell's temperament, and he was showing his frustration. A man who saw him in Richmond about this time said "he looked the wreck he was, his thin, narrow face, wizened and worn, twitched nervously, as did his hands and arms."[18]

Still, Dick was as combative as ever. Once, while on a tour of inspection with Lee, Anderson, and other leaders, Ewell's horse stumbled and down came both; it was an awful cropper. Dick was picked up and balanced on his one good leg. No bones had been broken but his head was terribly bruised and covered with blood. Lee instantly ordered him back to Richmond and told him to stay there until he was completely healed.

But just as he once used to sneak out with the skirmishers to get in the fight without his superiors knowing the risks he was taking, the old dragoon slipped back up to the lines only two or three hours after his mishap. And it was a painfully comical sight he presented! He had gone to a hospital, all right, where the physicians had swathed him in bandages from crown to shoulders. Two little apertures for his piercing eyes and two small breathing spaces were all that was left open for the lieutenant general. Quite indifferent, however, to his startling appearance, he was sharp about his work and lisping out directions to everyone in sight.[19]

Not many could maintain the spirit Ewell exhibited. The hardships were now too great and many men, as the bitter winter months dragged on, began to crack.

"Starvation, literal starvation, was doing its deadly work," General Gordon wrote. "So depleted and poisoned was the blood of many of Lee's men from insufficient and unsound food that a slight wound which would probably not have been reported at the beginning of the war would often cause blood poison, gangrene and death.

"It was a harrowing but not uncommon sight to see those hungry men gather the wasted corn from under the feet of half-fed horses and wash and parch and eat it to satisfy in some measure their craving for food."[20]

Other officers were noting in their reports to Lee on the destitution of their commands that some of their best men were showing evidence of temporary insanity, indifference to orders or to the consequences of disobedience—the natural and inevitable effects of their physical sufferings and the strain of the siege.

Desertions soared. Squads of men climbed out of their trenches and went over to the enemy at night; whole companies tried to head back to North Carolina or Georgia as armed units to avoid arrest. In a period of ten days in February, 1865, a total of 1,094 men left the lines and Lee was warning Richmond that he could not keep the army together unless examples were made. He meant executions, of course, but even that measure did not stem the desertion rate. The *esprit de corps* of a unit was often a factor in its absentee rate. During the same two weeks of March, while Pickett was reporting 512 men gone from his reorganized division of conscripts, Major General Joseph Kershaw was listing only 41 men missing from his fine First Corps division, the unit that had been led by Lafayette McLaws.

The one thin artery left to bring supplies to Lee's army,

now down to 40,000 men, was the rickety Southside Railroad. To start the spring campaign, Grant determined to sever it. He sent Sheridan's cavalry and a strong infantry force far beyond the Confederates' right in a sweeping end run for the railroad. Lee knew he could not permit the Union forces to reach the line; it would be the end for his army. He pulled Pickett's division out and ordered George, with Fitz Lee's cavalry, to get to the critical road juncture at Five Forks before Sheridan did. Pickett reached there in time, advanced to meet the Federals, got pushed back somewhat but still held the key intersection. Perhaps Lee, like Longstreet, also knew how important it was to make things quite plain to Pickett, for after the initial encounter he sent the Virginian a telegram reading:

"Hold Five Forks at all hazards. Protect road to Ford's Depot and prevent Union forces from striking the Southside Railroad. Regret exceedingly your forced withdrawal, and your inability to hold the advantage you had gained."[21]

Notwithstanding the critical situation, the next day, when no fighting erupted and he had convinced himself that the Union effort in his sector was over, Pickett did a remarkable thing. He decided to leave his troops and ride two miles to the rear to accept an invitation to a nice old-fashioned shad bake. The host for this pleasant interlude was cavalry General Tom Rosser. Fitzhugh Lee also was invited to share in Rosser's catch from the Nottoway River. Fitz, another good eater, could not resist and the two ranking officers rode off to lunch together.[22]

With the Confederate infantry commander and the cavalry commander in the sector thus out of sight and, because of the thick woods in the area, out of sound as well, Sheridan attacked. The leaders had been absent more than three hours. By the time they got back, the battle was virtually over and there was little direction they could give. Sheridan had struck like a thunderbolt and the hastily erected Rebel breastworks had been easily shattered. Pickett's troops, not men of the same mettle as those he had taken to Pennsylvania, were sent scurrying in all directions. More than 2,000 were taken prisoner. A blue horseman had almost bagged Pickett himself but George was so angry over what had befallen him that he yelled "damn you" at the Yank demanding his surrender, reeled his horse, and galloped off. Pickett's final demand on his men was to ask a few of them to risk their lives and hold off a Union force in another sector long enough for him to escape.

For his own part, Fitzhugh Lee—in greater disgrace for being the commanding general's nephew—could only say later, "I thought that the movements just there, for the time being, were suspended, and we were not expecting any attack that afternoon, as far as I know."[23]

Capitalizing on the momentum of the victory at Five Forks that suddenly rendered Petersburg untenable, Grant attacked A. P. Hill's Third Corps sector the next day in strong force and finally, after nine months of trying, succeeded in cracking the Petersburg line.

As Lee rode out to measure for himself the extent of the breakthrough, he said to an aide, "This is a sad business, colonel . . . it has happened as I told them in Richmond it would happen. The line has been stretched until it is broken."[24]

Only the day before, weak, sad-faced A. P. Hill had returned from a visit to the Confederate capital where he had spent some time with "fugee" relatives and had seen the lawlessness and the disorder that then prevailed there. Before he left, he was heard to say in reaction to some talk of how long it would be before the city would have to be evacuated, "I do not wish to survive the fall of Richmond."[25]

Hill was with Lee at the general's headquarters in the Turnbull house when he learned of the Union penetration and rushed out to his horse. He was trying to make his way to Harry Heth's headquarters, accompanied by Sergeant George W. Tucker, in charge of his couriers, when they encountered Yankee troops ahead of them on the road. The gray riders turned off and made a dash for the woods only to find a squad of bluecoats among the trees as they approached. Two soldiers had taken up positions behind a tree trunk and were training rifles on them.

"If you fire, you'll be swept to hell," Sergeant Tucker shouted at the men blocking their escape. "Our men are here. Surrender!"

Hill called out, "Surrender, you!"

But the Federals did not go for the ruse. Both men, members of the 138th Pennsylvania, fired at Hill who, though wearing a black cape over his uniform, was taken immediately for an officer of some rank. One bullet took off the general's thumb and then passed through his body near the heart. He fell to the ground, limbs outstretched. Sergeant Tucker caught the bridle of Hill's dappled-gray horse and galloped away with the mount to inform Lee that the commander of the Third Corps had been slain.[26]

When the commanding general, his lines collapsing around him, was told of Hill's death, he asked Colonel Palmer to convey the news to Dolly Hill as gently as possible. As the staff officer arrived at the cottage the Hills had been occupying, he could hear the voice of the general's beautiful young wife. She was singing as she carried on with her work, not knowing the desperate turn affairs had taken. For some reason, the colonel did not think to knock but simply let himself in, seemingly so as not to interrupt her abruptly. She heard his footsteps, the stirring at the door, and forgot her melody. When she approached the messenger, it was she who was the first to speak.

"The General's dead; you wouldn't be here unless he was dead."[27]

Of the 306 West Point graduates who had joined the Confederate forces, A. P. Hill was the seventy-second and the last to die during the war and the twenty-eighth of those who had been associated with Lee and the Virginia army.

At nightfall, after some time was bought by a Confederate suicide force that went in and held a key fort for several hours to detain the Yanks from pouring through the opening they had made in the Third Corps lines, the retreat from Petersburg and Richmond began.

"There was no sleeping in Petersburg that night," Douglas remembered, "no night except for the darkness. It was all commotion and bustle. While my brigade was waiting for its order to move, I rode to sundry homes to say good-bye. Before we got away, shells were bursting at places over the town and the air was now and then illuminated by the baleful light of mortars. The last person I spoke to in Petersburg was a young lady who afterwards became the wife of General W. H. F. Lee. She uttered not a word of fear or complaint. The infinite sadness of her silence was pathetic beyond words."[28]

As the troops at Petersburg pulled back westward over the bridges of the Appomattox, Richmond also was being abandoned and the forces there were blowing the spans over the James River to facilitate their escape.

Thousands of Confederates were bottlenecked at one bridge when Grant got within artillery range but he would not let his men fire on the Rebels. He said they would soon be captured and he didn't have the heart to turn guns on men in such a wretched state.

When the last man had gone over the last bridge from the capital, Joe Kershaw, on the west bank, called out to the engineers:

"All over. Good-bye. Blow her to hell."[29]

Along three different roads, the disintegrating Confederate Army retreated. One route was no better than another, for all led ultimately to the same little courthouse village.

At Sayler's Creek, Sheridan caught up with the forces of Ewell and Anderson and the remnant of Pickett's division and annihilated them. Ewell was taken prisoner along with Kershaw and five other generals. Sheridan wired Grant: "If the thing is pressed, I think Lee will surrender."[30] And even

Dick Ewell now thought that he should. He told his captors as he sat with other Confederate officers among the Federal leaders at Sheridan's campfire that night, the dim, flickering light making it difficult to discern blue fabric from gray:

"Our cause is gone. Lee should surrender now, before more lives are wasted."[31]

The old dragoon had little else to say. Finally motionless, he sat on the ground hugging his knee, his face bent down between his arms, and waited to be taken away to prison.

Dick Anderson also had had it. Coming upon the courtly South Carolinian after the catastrophe at Sayler's Creek, a brother officer was saddened to discover that Dick clearly had lost all heart for the cause and had become "the sad picture of a man who was whipped."[32]

Lee, even in his army's flight, could still remember to tend to organizational details. He dictated an order to an aide formally releasing both Anderson and Pickett from the army as supernumeraries, men for whom no commands suitable to their rank were available. Silently, without ceremony, as inconspicuous as he had tried to make his presence during his long service with the army, the modest Anderson slipped away and headed toward his home in far-off South Carolina and was spared the final scene. Pickett lingered and when Lee, sometime later, saw him riding along with the retreating army on the road to Appomattox, he asked contemptuously, "Is that man still with this army?"[33]

The reeling Rebels staggered on, desperately trying to shake loose the jackals snapping at them from all sides. With every mile without food or rest, the soldiers grew weaker and closer to collapse. The artillery horses could no longer pull the field pieces and many had to be abandoned. To keep himself going, Harry Heth remembered stealing a handful of corn from his horse and wondered as he munched on it how the enlisted men must be faring if he, a major general, had to eat forage.

Finally, a group of generals held a council of war without Lee and decided that, despite the articles of war, the time had come to tell the commander that the army could endure no more. They wanted Longstreet to carry the message.

"If General Lee doesn't know when to surrender until I tell him, he will never know," Dutch responded, predictably.[34]

At Appomattox Court House, the Federals got in front of the Rebel army and it was checkmated. Only hours before, they had captured the supplies that the Confederates had to have if they were to stand the remotest chance of pushing on and effecting a juncture with Joe Johnston. Lee had no other course but to ask for a meeting with General Grant.

While the two leaders sat and talked in the parlor of the Wilmer McLean house, generals from both sides began to congregate in front of the broad porch to wait and see what transpired. The tiny hamlet had been sealed off with sentries and the streets were quiet and deserted save for the growing cluster of gray- and blue-clad officers idling the time away in front of the frame building. As each brigadier or major general rode in, another almost-whispered reunion occurred, for each new arrival had known at least someone from the other side who was there.

Though they had long been separated, these men's get-togethers were not animated. Conversation was subdued in reverence to what was going on inside the house. All the leaders wore an air of anxiety. Many openly expressed the hope that the outcome would mean there would be no further need of bloodshed. All had had enough.

When Heth came in he was wearing a brand-new uniform. The Union General John Gibbon, a classmate with whom Harry had last shaken hands at Camp Floyd in distant Utah after the expedition against Brigham Young, commented on how handsomely dressed Harry was while everyone else there was looking so scruffy. Well, Harry explained, he had noticed the way the Yankees were capturing all the baggage trains and if he was going to lose his wardrobe, he preferred to save his new clothes rather than his patched outfits.[35] He could have added that being from a family of soldiers that had served Virginia since the French and Indian Wars, he had an innate sense that the moment called for some formality; but he would not have said it.

To those waiting outside, the time dragged slowly along. Conversation lagged. All heads turned, at one point, when some Federal officer called out, "There is Cadmus!"

Riding into the square on a sorry-looking old gray horse whose thin ribs showed the scant forage on which he had been subsisting came Cadmus Marcellus Wilcox, who had been one of the most popular men in the officer corps in the old service. For some reason, he was dressed in a long thick overcoat. After he had dismounted and clasped the hands of everyone in the group, someone asked the Tennessee bachelor about the need for a heavy overcoat in April. Was he ill? Cadmus grimly replied, "It's all I have." Opening the coat, he showed that a shirt was the only garment underneath. Pointing to a pair of saddle bags on his scrawny horse he said, "That's all the baggage I have left"; and turning to Sheridan, he remarked, "You have captured all the balance and you can't have that until you capture me!"[36]

When Lee came out of the house with his single aide, his step heavy on the creaking porch steps, they watched him slowly mount Traveller and sorrowfully trot off. It was apparent to his subalterns that he had accepted terms. The Union generals kept themselves in respectful control until he was gone and then let their joy at victory escape. Quickly the house was swarming with officers, those who could not fit into the small room anxiously soliciting those who had been present in the parlor for details of what took place. Long-haired George Custer emerged from the house with the small table on which the terms had been signed, a priceless souvenir for which he had given McLean $25. He rode off carrying the piece of furniture over his head like a trophy.

A group of his old cronies—Rufus Ingalls and Merritt, Sheridan and Gibbon—surrounded Cadmus after a while and made him their special prisoner, marching him in his pathetic attire to meet Grant again; and Sam was visibly pleased to see him.

When the excitement subsided a bit, the officers retreated to the nearby tavern—to talk, to drink and, for some, to work out the details of the paroling of the 28,000 men Lee had surrendered. Gordon, who had had to abandon his wife at Petersburg when the army evacuated though she had given birth to their third child only a day before, was among them. Someone remembered the scarred Georgian saying that he would have been ready to surrender sooner if he knew the Rebs would be received so magnanimously.

Heth had also come over to the tavern and was heard to express the feeling that he would rather have had to fight the politicians who brought on the war than the soldiers arrayed against him. Before Harry left the scene, Grant would have a gift for him and never was a more suitable and thoughtful present offered: It was two gallons of good whiskey.[37]

Pickett also was still around. But there was no backslapping or friendly greetings from the men in blue for him. The Kinston executions had been well publicized and there was resentment that George was being allowed to go free. In fact, some of the Union soldiers were offended that any of the West Pointers were being paroled. As one of Sheridan's officers put it, "There was . . . not a little chagrin in some quarters that Pickett and other officers of distinction who were deserters from the United States service at the outbreak of the war should be allowed the same generous terms accorded the others."[38]

Perhaps the most touching reunion that took place among the old chums was Grant's encounter with Longstreet. He had last seen Dutch on the streets of St. Louis long before the war. Sam had been down on his luck at that time but, in his fashion, insisted on repaying on the spot a small sum he had owed Longstreet. The money had been reluctantly accepted. Stubborn old Sam: A debt's a debt and all that. Both were still busy with the details of the surrender when first they ran into one another in the hall of the

McLean house but Sam did have time to thrust a cigar at Longstreet and thump him on the back. Later, when their duties to their respective governments were discharged, Grant threw an arm around his sturdy comrade and growled, "Pete, let's go back to the good old times and play a game of brag as we used to."[39]

It was finished.

11

"Those of Us Who Are Left Behind"

THE WAR WAS OVER but a struggle just as bitter now began for the regular army officers who had thrown in with the Confederacy. Not unlike lawyers disbarred or physicians deprived of their licenses to practice, they were suddenly without professions, outcasts forced to enter some totally new endeavor to meet their family responsibilities, and all too aware of how ill-equipped they were for any life other than the military. To make matters worse, after the war there were few Southerners who, however much they may have wished to help their revered officers reestablish themselves in new careers, were in a position to extend any aid. They would have to shift for themselves, and without the aura their gold-gilded gray tunics had given them, to compete in a wrecked, confused economic climate with the orderlies who had once held their mounts, with the ruined landowners, and with the young and the commercially schooled.

When only a few years after the war someone discovered "Dick" Anderson, he who had been a lieutenant general in Lee's army, swinging a pick as a day laborer in the Charleston yards of the Southern Central Railroad, some awareness was created of just how difficult things were for these forlorn misfits.

Anderson, class of '42, had returned from Virginia to Hill Crest, his ancestral home, to find it dilapidated, debt-ridden, and deserted. To restore and maintain the place, the former corps commander–turned–farmer tried to cultivate a nearby plantation but, because of his lack of knowledge, completely failed. He went to Charleston for work of any sort, rung by rung lowering his standards, but could find nothing. One day, a railroad work gang was being formed. He took a place on line, and someone handed General Anderson a tool. When the president of the railroad learned who it was he had re-placing ties for him, he quickly transferred Anderson to a clerical position that was hardly less degrading. Eventually, Anderson gained the lofty post of railroad agent for the town of Camden but lost even this dreary position because of the dishonesty of an employee under him. Once more this man who had been responsible for thousands of men's lives in combat was without the means to preserve his own and his family's in peacetime. The governor of South Carolina, the state that had long ago awarded Anderson a silver sword for his service in Mexico, now pretended to come to the aid of the destitute general, making him a state phosphate inspec-tor. He later explained with some remorse that it was the best position he had at his disposal.[1]

Things went very badly for Heth, as well, for some time. His family's coal mining interests near Richmond were idle and he turned initially, like so many others with a familiar name to get them inside a door, to the insurance field. It was no Southerner who got Harry on his feet, finally. It was his old classmate at the Point, Ambrose Burnside. Luck had turned Burnside's way, and the man who had been such a big loser found shortly after the war a political charm that got him elected governor of the state of Rhode Island. Harry needed help and Burnside, being the man he was, knew he had to do something. He certainly could not receive him at the state capitol; instead, he arranged a rendezvous at a New York City hotel. They talked things over. For sure, something must have been said about Powell Hill. And then the commitment came: Reopen the Heth mines and I'll honor whatever drafts you need to write, Burnside said—and it was no prank. The offer was gratefully accepted and Harry had his new start.[2]

Some of Lee's officers became mercenaries, going to far-off countries to fight in causes in which they had no interest but where at least they would be able to retain the level of authority to which they had advanced. Charles Field, the old 2nd U.S. Cavalry lieutenant who had surrendered the largest organized infantry unit at Appomattox, donned a fez and accepted a high post in the army of the Khedive of Egypt.[3] Others went to Mexico to serve Maximillian's short-lived empire. Cadmus Wilcox was among them. When he arrived, they offered him the rank of *chef d'bataillon* in the emperor's French army. That will not do, responded the man who had let Lee, himself, know when he thought it was time he was made a major general. Cadmus would settle for nothing less than general of brigade with these foreigners. The empire collapsed while Cadmus waited in a hotel room for his price to be met, and perhaps that saved his neck. During his stay in Mexico, Wilcox became something of a guide for other ex-Confederates, showing them the old battlefields of the Mexican War and explaining the engagements in detail. He pointed out on his tours, no doubt, the aqueduct he had daringly mounted under fire as a brazen young lieutenant to signal to the army the capture of the Bolen gate during the siege of Mexico City. How long ago it must have seemed to him! Quite an expert on the Mexican campaigns was old Cadmus Marcellus: Though he would put few lines on paper about his Civil War experiences, he would write a history of the Mexican War that would stand for decades as the definitive work.[4]

Dick Ewell and the other generals captured at Sayler's Creek and Five Forks in the closing days of the war had been taken to Fort Warren in Boston before the surrender was made at Appomattox. While the new administration, embittered by the assassination of Lincoln, was reconsidering what sort of treatment to accord the Rebel generals, they were kept in confinement for up to six months. Despite Ewell's poor physical condition, he was put off by himself in a damp stone cell. There is no telling how long he might have been retained as a prisoner had not his aggressive wife Lizinka, using all her brass and political influence, let out a sustained scream for his release. To the President of the United States, whom she had known well in Tennessee, she did not hesitate to say, "If Richard dies in Fort Warren, how I will hate you— wicked as it is to hate anyone." She signed her letter, "Your miserable friend."[5]

Once released, Ewell, physically shattered, retired to one of "Mrs. Brown's" still prosperous farms in Tennessee where he lived very comfortably and helped increase the reputation of the lands as among the best managed in the country. He lived only to 1872, his death coming twenty-four hours after the funeral of his protective wife. On his death-bed, the old dragoon solicited a promise that "If any stone or shaft is ever raised over me, take care that nothing reflecting against the government of the United States is put upon it."[6]

John Bell Hood's life after the war was as melancholy as Anderson's. He had gone home a broken man. A young lady with whose family the deposed lieutenant general made the journey remembered his sorry state:

"I can see him now, we were in the baggage car, seated on boxes and trunks in all the misery and discomfort of the time. He sat opposite and with calm, sad eyes looked out on the passing scenes, apparently noting nothing. The cause he loved was lost, he was overwhelmed with humiliation at the utter failure of his leadership. In the face of his misery, which was greater than our own, we sat silent. There seemed no comfort anywhere."[7]

Two years after the war, Hood married and for a time he was very successful as a merchant in New Orleans, but some foolish, rash ventures soon forced him into poverty. In 1879, when only 48, Hood died of smallpox. Six days before, his wife had succumbed to the disease. The general simply did not have the means to leave the city as so many others had done to avoid the epidemic. To support his nine orphaned children, someone collected Hood's memoirs and published them under the very appropriate title, *Advance and Retreat.*

Jubal Early, disguised as a farmer, also had made his way across the country after Appomattox bound for Mexico and swearing that he would never live under the U.S. flag. But Jube, for all his barking, soon changed his mind and came back to Franklin County. In a few years, he became one of the more prosperous of the ex-Confederates though not in a way to be greatly admired.

For a salary variously estimated to be between $12,000 and $30,000 a year, both astronomical figures in those days, he let his name be used as a commissioner to give an air of honesty and respectability to the notoriously corrupt Louisiana Lottery. A writer observing him at one of the drawings noted that Early "still affects gray cloth and with his patriarchal beard and stoop certainly has a saintly look as he sits on the platform and calls off 'fortune's favorites.' "[8] People who disliked Early during the war could now, in the misery of Reconstruction, genuinely despise him for his lucrative position. A South Carolina officer saw him this way:

"He continued to pose after the war and was very harsh in his criticism of men who certainly did as good service as he did. He denounced their errors mercilessly, while he and Beauregard were complacently earning enormous salaries by serving as decoys for the Louisiana Lottery." It was the popular view.[9]

Two months after Appomattox, the Federal government indicted George Pickett for the Kinston executions. Upon learning of the action he gathered up his teen-aged wife, LaSalle, and a few belongings, fled across the border to Canada, and took up lodging in a Montreal rooming house. He even used an assumed name, Edwards. From these secure, remote digs, he began appealing to friends in the government by mail to have the charges against him quashed. To

Grant, whom he knew from his service in the Northwest, Pickett employed a manner far different from that he assumed during the incident. Now came phrases like "I acted simply as the general commanding the department." He pleaded for some assurance from Grant that he, Pickett, would "not be disturbed in my endeavors to keep my family from starvation."[10]

It was a touchy situation for Sam. On behalf of the besieged Pickett, Grant wrote to President Johnson a recommendation for clemency or, if that was out of the question, at least a directive not to bring Pickett to trial. By the tenor of his letter, it would appear that Grant had no great concern for Pickett, the man, but was more interested in living up to the terms of surrender he had offered to Lee and which had been accepted. The conditions made no mention of one of Lee's officers to be placed under arrest for atrocities.

"General Pickett I know personally to be an honorable man," Grant advised the Chief Executive, "but in this case his judgment prompted him to do what cannot well be sustained, though I do not see how good, either to the friends of the deceased or by fixing an example for the future can be secured by his trial now."[11]

Grant's letter, for all intents and purposes, closed the matter and George and his flowing locks were soon in evidence once more about Richmond. He too went into the insurance business.

Only once after the war, in 1870, did Pickett meet General Lee again and that was in a room at a Richmond hotel where Lee, now president of Washington University, was stopping. It was Major John Mosby, the raider, who had learned Lee was in the city and mentioned it to George. Pickett's response was strange. He said that if Mosby would accompany him, he would call and pay his respects to the general, but he did not want to be alone with him. Mosby acceded.

"The interview was cold and formal and evidently embarrassing to both," Mosby recalled. After but a few minutes

Mosby got up to leave, as did George, and they left the hotel together. As soon as they were alone, Pickett began to speak bitterly of his former commander, rudely calling him "that old man." Soon he blurted out what he really wanted to say:

"He had my division massacred at Gettysburg."

Mosby said his response was: "Well, it made you immortal."[12] One wonders with what inflection he phrased the reply.

Pickett was not the only Confederate leader whom Grant helped get out of trouble. When he became President, he began dispensing Federal positions to those in need and the plights of many were improved. After him, President Grover Cleveland also found places in the government for the Confederate generals and for many years there was something of a colony of Lee's officers in Washington: James Longstreet, Harry Heth, Fitzhugh Lee, and Charley Field were among them. For decades, Cadmus Wilcox was a familiar figure on the Washington social scene while earning his living as a messenger and later acting assistant doorkeeper of the U.S. Senate.

Ten years after Appomattox, four old grads who had worn the gray came back to West Point as full-fledged members of the newly organized Graduates Association. The Rebel contingent was made up of Francis H. Smith, '33, the long-time superintendent of the Virginia Military Institute that had provided so many capable officers to the Confederacy; Joseph R. Anderson, '36, the brigadier general who had reluctantly given up field service to undertake the far more important responsibility of directing the Tredegar Iron Works, the South's primary producer of artillery and ammunition; Eugene E. McLean of the distinguished class of '42 who had served primarily in the quartermaster department; and his far more famous classmate whom the plebes probably scurried to aid with his baggage out of consideration for his obviously useless right arm—James Longstreet. The length of their journeys was evidence enough of the intensity of their desire to view once more the scenes of their youth, and to reflect upon old chums and what had become of them.

Unhappily but not unexpectedly there was something of a falling-out among the Confederate leaders after the war, one which began at about the time most had reestablished themselves in some form of regular employment and could afford the time to write their versions of how and why their army had been defeated. Once the name-calling and the blame-placing started it spread infectiously, and soon the former comrades-in-arms were battling furiously among themselves but with pens rather than swords.

The controversy seemed always to center on Gettysburg; it apparently began in 1873 when, at the dedication of the Lee Chapel in Lexington, Virginia, Bishop William N. Pendleton, who had been chief of artillery in the Army of Northern Virginia, used the occasion to deliver a sharp criticism of Longstreet, going so far as to blame him for the failure of the campaign. By word of mouth and by newspaper accounts, Pendleton's remarks circulated throughout the South, no doubt distorted and exaggerated.

That it should be Pendleton, of all people, who would cast the first stone at Longstreet was a shock to a number of people who knew him, including Colonel Thomas Goree, who had served on Dutch's staff long and faithfully. Reacting to the charges, he wrote:

"It does seem preposterous and absurd to me, and must to any soldier of the army of Virginia, the idea of such an old granny as Pendleton presuming to give a lecture as knowing anything about the battle of Gettysburg. Although nominally chief of artillery, yet he was in the actual capacity of ordnance officer and I believe miles in the rear. I know that I did not see him on the field during the battle. It was a notorious fact and generally remarked that he was almost entirely ignored by General Lee as chief of artillery and the management of it given to the corps chiefs of artillery."[13]

Longstreet replied to the bishop's charges in an article

published in the Philadelphia *Times* but this only sparked new criticisms from Fitzhugh Lee. While Dutch was beating off that assault, Jubal Early, John B. Gordon, and Samuel French, a Confederate general and West Pointer from New Jersey, were busy preparing their briefs on what had gone wrong and again Longstreet would be made the main culprit. Early? Why, he was nothing but "a marplot and a disturber" and most decidedly Lee's weakest general, Longstreet counterattacked.[14] Soon the popular *Century Magazine* would be making the Gettysburg controversy a regular monthly feature, printing the opinions of virtually everyone involved in the campaign all the way down to Lafayette McLaws's body servant.

Longstreet could be ridiculed with impunity because he had greatly offended the unreconstructed Rebs by becoming a Republican and a functionary of the Scalawag government in New Orleans, where he had settled. He suffered additionally in this war of the quill when, feeling in need of reinforcements in the form of a ghost writer, he chose a former lieutenant in a Union Negro regiment to do his phrasing.

But he was by no means the only one of Lee's subalterns to be held responsible for the outcome of the crucial campaign. Few were spared. When Harry Heth ventured to attribute the loss in part to Jeb Stuart's absence, John Mosby replied cuttingly that it wasn't the absence of cavalry that caused the defeat but, "I would rather say, it was due to the presence of Heth."[15]

Mosby was not alone in attacking Heth for his role at Gettysburg, where he had committed the army to a major battle by attacking the Union First Corps with his full division before Lee could assemble and choose his ground; and for his role at Falling Waters, where in command of the rear guard he was unable to protect the army's recrossing of the Potomac and suffered the loss of some five hundred prisoners. Unfortunately, Harry was not one who could ignore the accusations. He took them very much to heart and became extremely unhappy in later years as he developed the conviction that he was being blamed personally for the army's defeat.

When they went after Ewell, Dick knew better how to handle them. He said openly that "it took a dozen blunders to lose the battle of Gettysburg and I committed a good many of them." And he said no more.[16]

Not only were the West Pointers fighting among themselves but there were those in the South still convinced that the academy bunch, as a whole, was the root cause of their failure.

A Virginia railroad engineer named W. W. Blackford who had utilized his skills to become an outstanding army engineer officer would write somewhat bitterly, when it was all over, "Our cause died of West Point as much as any one thing."[17]

And he offered a case, one based on long association with the academy graduates. The full brief for his side deserves to be heard.

The average West Pointer, Blackford averred, "who had reached the age of forty in the discharge of the duties of the army officer, in time of peace, is worthless in war. Of course there are brilliant exceptions in both the Northern and Southern armies, but they are exceptions. They are brought up to think that after graduating at West Point there is nothing left for them in this world to learn and twenty years' garrison life in the West, in contact with inferiors, and with nothing to stimulate to exertion, leaves them selfish, narrow-minded, and bigoted. To look at the numbers in our army, and then to count those who were even moderately successful as soldiers, one is astonished at the smallness of the proportion; and still more is this astonishment increased when we count how many were absolutely disastrous failures.

"The same number of graduates from our best colleges, who had never opened a military book at equal ages with the West Pointers, and taken from the successful businessmen of the country and placed in the same positions at the beginning of the war would, in my opinion, have done better on the average. The young men from West Point, who had to win their way and had not been fossilized by garrison or bureau life, as a rule did splendidly, those of thirty and under, say. The 'old soldiers' are so intensely jealous of each other; they look at everything through green glasses! The country or their cause is nothing to them when opposed to their feelings, and it is so deeply seated that they really are not aware of its existence, I verily believe, in many cases. Then, when high in rank, some of them are so afraid of losing their reputation that they won't take the risks necessary in war, and avoid a battle they are not certain of winning, when the chances are still in their favor."[18]

Much of the animosity concerning the "old army" regulars was directed toward Lee himself. In probably the most scathing denunciation of the man that a Southerner ever dared put into print, a South Carolina colonel would write long after the war of the conflict between the professional soldiers and the volunteer officers that Lee had fueled:

"He had an apparent antipathy to anything partaking of pomposity and the vanity of war, but he had an utterly undue regard for the elementary teachings of West Point and for the experience gained by the very small police duty of our miniature regular army.

"He failed to realize that while a military school is excellent for the training of drill masters, who are most necessary, it teaches little of military science in comparison with the hard experience of a single campaign."[19]

William Mahone, a V.M.I. graduate and railroad builder who in the Confederate service had become a division commander, reflected on Lee and his manner of command and left many who had served with him something to ponder:

"He was the most [handsome] specimine [sic] and proudest man I ever saw. He had no appreciation of a joke. Polite, but stern and matter of fact in all things. His long service in the regular army had left him with a reverence for authority and a rigid respect for rules and regulations which were unfortunate and hurt full [sic] for one in command of an army of revolution. He should have gone to the field unfettered and his mere [wish] should have been the law."[20]

By and large, in the postwar struggle for survival the nonprofessional soldiers who had made names for themselves in the army fared much better than the West Pointers. Among the exceptions were Fitzhugh Lee, who became governor of Virginia, and the badly crippled Francis Nicholls, who was elected governor of Louisiana and as such broke up the corrupt lottery; they became the only members of the "old army" crowd that served under Lee to reach genuinely high civil office, whereas John B. Gordon, Billy Mahone, Wade Hampton, and other volunteers who became generals reached the U.S. Senate. Gordon was for decades the most demanded speaker at any dedication or commemoration related to the Army of Northern Virginia and headed many veterans' organizations, posing frequently for the camera but always with his face turned to avoid showing the disfigurement he suffered at Antietam. The explanation is by no means difficult to find, for the very qualities that carried these men to the top of Lee's command system in the face of the West Pointers' competition—their magnetism, bearing, ambition, and, probably most of all, adaptability—carried them through the awful despair and turmoil of Reconstruction.

Joseph Kershaw of South Carolina is a good example. A lawyer by trade, he had—by high intelligence, personality, and fine bearing in combat—gradually advanced in the army until by 1865 he was one of the most competent major generals left with Lee. He too had been captured at Sayler's Creek and was taken with Dick Ewell, Bushrod Johnson and other generals to Fort Warren (a journey none would have completed alive had not their Union guards succeeded in convincing an angry mob in Providence, Rhode Island that the Rebel prisoners in their care were only a group of blockade runners). Kershaw finally returned to his Camden home in June, two months after Appomattox, without a dollar to his name. To pay the taxes on his home he had to sell the family's jewelry and even its candlesticks. Yet before the year was out he had resumed his political career and had won election to the state senate, and in a few years became a circuit court judge.

Perhaps the army men lacked the drive, the zest, the incentive to come out on top in the struggle to rebuild the South. Whatever the reason, scores of these men who had commanded brigades and divisions of infantry in battle finished out their lives as freight agents, tax collectors, small town police chiefs and, of all things, postmasters. Some became educators and a few of these attained positions of note. Daniel Harvey Hill miraculously survived the war to become president of the University of Arkansas.

The joys of their late years were few for the West Pointers and among the more cherished was to be remembered by their men: to be paid a visit by a former aide or to be invited to attend a brigade reunion, where they might hear the tinny little bands play "Dixie" and the veterans, now leading lives as dull as their own, try to recapture the Rebel yell.

Lafayette McLaws, commander of the division that had played the key role in the defensive victory at Fredericksburg and contributed so much to the triumph at Chancellorsville in the army's glory days, returned to Savannah after the war and for a number of years was the postmaster there until "turned out of office by Mr. [Chester] Arthur, General Grant's influence not being great enough with that president to keep me in office." In 1890, though then sixty-nine, the old soldier "being without permanent occupation" and in need of "any duty that would keep me employed constantly under pay" applied unsuccessfully for a position with the Chicago World's Fair Commission, saying he was ready to relocate wherever necessary.[21] When he expired seven years later there was discussion of what inscription to place on a monument for the much-abused major general, until one former soldier came up with a line with which McLaws could not have been more pleased. It was simply, "He knew where to lead us and always brought us out."

By 1900 they were almost all gone, Lee's generals. Longstreet was among the last to depart, passing away in 1904. In his last years he lived far from the storm of controversy in a small house in Gainesville, Georgia, recognizable by a crudely lettered sign that read "good home made wine sold cheap." Veterans from the old First Corps often stopped by to pay their respects to "Old Peter," a sad figure now with a black patch over one eye after a cancer operation. Though his enemies in the South formed against him in legions, few men who had ever served under him joined their ranks.

When Cadmus Wilcox died in Washington, eight former generals served as pallbearers at his funeral, four of them from the Confederate army and four who had worn the blue.

Only two generals from the Army of Northern Virginia who had come out of West Point were ever permitted to serve in the United States Army again. When the Spanish-American War broke out, Fitzhugh Lee and Tom Rosser, both cavalry leaders, were given commissions as generals of U.S. Volunteers. Joe Wheeler of the Army of Tennessee was also readmitted to the federal service. All the others, however, had to pay for the rest of their lives the price of the defeat of that cause they had relinquished so much to support. When their melancholy ends are considered, one can more readily understand what Lee must have been envisioning when he said, upon learning of the fall of A. P. Hill on that last day at Petersburg:

"He is at rest now and those of us who are left behind are the ones to suffer."[22]

Appendix—
The Roll

Graduates of the United States Military Academy who served in the Confederate armies, by class and class rank, with those who died while in the service of the Confederacy indicated by asterisk:

1814
Lewis G. DeRussy (6)

1815
William H. Chase (30)
Samuel Cooper (36)

1817
Richard B. Lee (9)
Angus W. McDonald (13)

1820
Edward G. Butler (9)
* John H. Winder (11)

1821
* Charles Dimmock (5)

1822
Walter Gwynn (8)
Isaac R. Trimble (17)

1825
* Daniel S. Donelson (5)

1825, cont.
Benjamin Huger (8)
Nathaniel H. Street (23)

1826
* Albert S. Johnston (8)
Edward B. White (9)
Francis L. Dancy (10)
* John B. Grayson (22)
John Archer (25)

1827
* James Bradford (4)
* Leonidas Polk (8)
George J. Rains (13)

1828
Hugh W. Mercer (3)
* Joseph L. Locke (8)
Jefferson Davis (23)
Thomas F. Drayton (28)

1829
Robert E. Lee
Joseph E. Johnsto   )
A. G. Blanchard (2t
Theophilus Holmes (44)

1830
William N. Pendleton (5)
John B. Magruder (15)
Albert I. Bledsoe (16)
Meriwether L. Clark (23)
Lloyd J. Beall (25)
* William C. Heyward (26)

1831
Albert M. Lea (5)
Lucius B. Northrup (22)
James S. Williams (28)

1832
Benjamin S. Ewell (3)
* Philip St. G. Cocke (6)
Richard G. Fain (20)
George B. Crittenden (26)
Robert H. Archer (33)
Robert G. Gatlin (35)
Humphrey Marshall (42)

1833
Francis H. Smith (5)
* David B. Harris (7)
James L. Davis (16)
Abraham C. Myers (32)
Daniel Ruggles (34)
Benjamin E. DuBose (39)

1834
Robert Allen (5)
William T. Stockton (8)
Charles A. Fuller (10)
James F. Cooper (17)
Thomas O. Barnwell (23)
Goode Bryan (25)

1835
Arnoldus V. Brumby (7)
William H. Griffin (27)
Peter C. Gaillard (29)

1835, cont.
James M. Wells (39)
Jones M. Withers (44)
Larkin Smith (47)
* Hugh McLeod (56)

1836
Danville Leadbetter (3)
Joseph R. Anderson (4)
Christopher Q. Tompkins (27)
* Lloyd Tilghman (46)

1837
Braxton Bragg (5)
William W. Mackall (8)
* Robert T. Jones (13)
Jubal A. Early (18)
Edward Bradford (19)
John C. Pemberton (27)
Arthur M. Rutledge (32)
Arnold Elzey (33)
* W. H. T. Walker (46)
Robert H. Chilton (48)

1838
P. G. T. Beauregard (2)
James H. Trapier (3)
William B. Blair (11)
Henry C. Wayne (14)
Milton A. Haynes (18)
William J. Hardee (26)
Henry H. Sibley (31)
Edward Johnson (32)
Alexander W. Reynolds (35)
Carter L. Stevenson (42)

1839
Jeremy F. Gilmer (4)
Alexander R. Lawton (13)
* Charles Wickliffe (26)

1840
Paul O. Hebert (1)
William Gilham (5)
John P. McCown (10)
Richard S. Ewell (13)

1840, cont.
James G. Martin (14)
Bushrod R. Johnson (23)
* Reuben P. Campbell (27)
William Steele (31)
Robert P. Maclay (32)
Thomas Jordan (41)

1841
* Smith Stansbury (4)
Josiah Gorgas (6)
Sewall L. Fremont (17)
Samuel Anderson (18)
Samuel Jones (19)
* Robert S. Garnett (27)
* Richard B. Garnett (29)
Claudius W. Sears (31)
* John M. Jones (39)
Edward Murray (41)
Abraham Buford (51)

1842
George W. Rains (3)
Gustavus W. Smith (8)
Mansfield Lovell (9)
A. P. Stewart (12)
Martin L. Smith (16)
Daniel H. Hill (28)
Armistead Rust (31)
Richard H. Anderson (40)
George W. Lay (41)
E. E. McLean (47)
Lafayette McLaws (48)
* Earl Van Dorn (52)
James Longstreet (54)

1843
Roswell S. Ripley (7)
Samuel G. French (14)
Franklin Gardner (17)
Edmund B. Holloway (19)

1844
Daniel M. Frost (4)
* Francis J. Thomas (6)
Simon B. Buckner (11)

1845
* W. H. C. Whiting (1)
Louis Hebert (3)
Thomas G. Rhett (6)
Edmund Kirby Smith (25)
James M. Hawes (29)
Richard Radford (31)
* Bernard E. Bee (33)

1846
John A. Brown (16)
* Thomas J. Jackson (17)
* John Adams (25)
* W. D. Smith (35)
Dabney H. Maury (37)
* David R. Jones (41)
Cadmus M. Wilcox (54)
William M. Gardner (55)
Samuel B. Maxey (58)
George E. Pickett (59)

1847
Daniel M. Beltzhoover (12)
* Ambrose P. Hill (15)
Edward D. Blake (37)
Henry Heth (38)

1848
Walter H. Stevens (4)
* William E. Jones (10)
William G. Gill (12)
Thomas S. Rhett (14)
Charles H. Tyler (23)
* John C. Booth (24)
Thomas K. Jackson (25)
William N. R. Beall (30)
William T. Mechling (33)
Nathan G. Evans (36)
George H. Steuart (37)

1849
* Johnson K. Duncan (5)
John C. Moore (17)
John Withers (23)
Beverly H. Robertson (25)
Charles W. Field (27)

1849, cont.
Seth M. Barton (28)
Duff C. Green (29)
Thomas G. Williams (32)
Thornton A. Washington (33)
John W. Frazer (34)
Alfred Cumming (39)
Samuel H. Reynolds (42)
* James McIntosh (43)

1850
Jacob Culbertson (7)
Achilles Bowen (10)
* William T. Magruder (11)
James P. Flewellen (14)
* Lucius M. Walker (15)
Armstead L. Long (17)
Robert Ransom (18)
* Charles S. Winder (22)
Nicholas B. Pearce (26)
* William R. Calhoun (27)
Robert Johnston (28)
Thomas Bingham (29)
William L. Cabell (33)
James H. Wilson (34)
Robert G. Cole (37)
* John Mouton (38)
James L. Corley (40)
Donald C. Stith (44)

1851
William T. Welcker (4)
Caleb Huse (7)
* Benjamin H. Helm (9)
* Junius Daniel (33)
Melancthon Smith (36)
Edward A. Palfrey (37)
John T. Shaaff (38)
Lawrence S. Baker (42)

1852
Joseph C. Ives (5)
* George B. Anderson (10)
Henry DeVeuve (12)
George R. Cosby (17)
Robert B. Thomas (18)

1852, cont.
* Matthew L. Davis (21)
John H. Forney (22)
Marshall T. Polk (23)
Charles H. Rundell (25)
Philip Stockton (33)
Arthur P. Bagby (39)
Richard V. Bonneau (42)

1853
William R. Boggs (4)
* John S. Bowen (13)
James L. White (25)
Benjamin Allston (26)
John R. Chambliss (31)
Henry B. Davidson (33)
Henry H. Walker (41)
John Bell Hood (44)
James A. Smith (45)
Thomas M. Jones (47)
* Lucius L. Rich (50)
* Reuben H. Ross (51)

1854
G. W. C. Lee (1)
* James Deshler (7)
* John Pegram (10)
Charles G. Rogers (11)
* James E. B. Stuart (13)
Archibald Gracie (14)
Stephen D. Lee (17)
* W. Dorsey Pender (19)
* John B. Villepigue (22)
Abner Smead (25)
John O. Long (31)
* John T. Mercer (40)
John Mullins (43)
* Horace Randal (45)

1855
Frederick L. Childs (9)
Francis R. T. Nicholls (12)
Francis A. Shoup (15)
John R. Church (16)
James H. Hill (23)
* Robert C. Hill (33)

1856

* Charles C. Lee (4)
Hylan B. Lyon (19)
Lunsford L. Lomax (21)
James P. Major (23)
George Jackson (30)
* Frank S. Armistead (34)
William H. Jackson (38)
* Owen K. McLemore (39)
Fitzhugh Lee (45)
Arthur S. Cunningham (49)

1857

* Richard K. Meade (2)
E. Porter Alexander (3)
William P. Smith (9)
Thomas J. Berry (11)
* Oliver H. Fish (13)
Samuel W. Ferguson (19)
Manning M. Kimmel (22)
George A. Cunningham (25)
Henry C. McNeill (26)
Aurelius F. Cone (28)
Paul J. Quattlebaum (29)
John S. Marmaduke (30)
George W. Holt (31)
Robert H. Anderson (35)
* Lafayette Peck (38)

1858

* Moses J. White (2)
* Joseph Dixon (3)
William H. Echols (4)
John S. Saunders (5)
James H. Hallonquist (6)
Leroy Napier (10)

1858, cont.

Solomon Williams (11)
* Richard H. Brewer (12)
Andrew Jackson (15)
Bryan M. Thomas (22)
William G. Robinson (25)

1859

Samuel H. Lockett (2)
* Charles R. Collins (3)
* Robert F. Beckham (6)
Moses H. Wright (7)
Joseph Wheeler (19)

1860

Benjamin Sloan (7)
* William H. McCreery (11)
* S. Dodson Ramseur (14)
* John M. Kerr (19)
John R. B. Burtwell (24)
Wade H. Gibbes (28)
Frank Huger (31)
Edward Riley (34)
Harold Borland (41)

MAY 1861

L. G. Hexton (6)
Nathaniel R. Chambliss (9)
* Charles E. Patterson (16)
Charles C. Campbell (24)
Olin F. Rice (41)
Mathias W. Henry (44)

JUNE 1861

Clarence Derrick (4)
George O. Watts (32)
Frank A. Reynolds (35)

Notes

Foreword

1. Determined from individual service records contained in G. W. Cullum's "Biographical Register of the Officers and Graduates of the Unites States Military Academy from 1802 to 1867"; and augmented by Ellsworth Eliot, Jr. in "West Point in the Confederacy."
2. George E. Pickett, *Heart of a Soldier,* letters compiled and edited by LaSalle Corbell Pickett, 49.

Chapter 1:
"It Is a Good Cause"

1. Francis Paul Prucha, "Distribution of Regular Troops Before the Civil War," *Military Affairs* (1952), 169–73.
2. Dabney H. Maury, *Recollections of a Virginian in the Mexican, Indian and Civil Wars,* 76.
3. R. E. Lee letter to Anna Maria Fitzhugh, Sept. 8, 1857, Duke University.
4. Maury, 103.
5. John B. Hood, *Advance and Retreat,* 6.
6. James Longstreet, *From Manassas to Appomattox,* 29.
7. Philip H. Sheridan, *Personal Memoirs,* 121.
8. Official Records of the Union and Confederate Armies, I, Part 1, 503–79. (Cited hereafter as O.R.)

9. Morris Schaff, *The Spirit of Old West Point*, 196.
10. William Dorsey Pender, *The General to His Lady*, 15.
11. E. Porter Alexander, *Military Memoirs of a Confederate*, 6.
12. Schaff, 220.
13. Sidney Forman, *A History of the U.S. Military Academy*, 16.
14. Maury, 132.
15. Douglas Southall Freeman, *Lee's Lieutenants*, II, 145–46. (Citing John R. Cooke mss., J. E. B. Stuart to Cooke, Jan. 18, 1862.)
16. A. R. Hancock, *Reminiscences of Winfield Scott Hancock*, 69.
17. Longstreet, 30.
18. Ibid., 30.
19. George E. Pickett, *Soldier of the South*, a later edition of letters to his wife, edited by Arthur Crew Inman, 5–6.
20. Lafayette McLaws Papers.
21. James W. Ratchford, *Some Reminiscences of Persons and Anecdotes of the Civil War*, 19–20.
22. Thomas J. Fleming, *West Point—The Men and Times of the U.S.M.A.*, 166–67.
23. Ibid., 167.
24. *Henry Heth Memoirs*, edited by James L. Morrison, Jr., 152.
25. Aurelia Austin, *Georgia Boys with Stonewall Jackson*, xi.
26. Francis Trevelyn Miller, editor, *The Photographic History of the Civil War*, Vol. VIII, 129.
27. Richard O'Connor, *Hood: Cavalier General*, 61.
28. Maury, 50.
29. G. Moxley Sorrel, *Recollections of a Confederate Staff Officer*, 31.
30. George C. Eggleston, *A Rebel's Recollections*, 136.
31. John O. Casler, *Four Years in the Stonewall Brigade*, 25.
32. Randolph A. Shotwell, *The Papers of . . .* , edited by J. G. de R. Hamilton, 170.
33. Randolph H. McKim, *A Soldier's Recollections*, 41.

Chapter 2:
"The Entente Cordiale"

1. Edward A. Moore, *The Story of a Cannoneer Under Stonewall Jackson*, 45.
2. John H. Worsham, *One of Jackson's Foot Cavalry*, 206.

3. Southern Historical Society Papers, XIII, 259 (cited hereafter as SHSP).

4. Henry Steele Commager, *The Blue and the Gray*, I, 138. (From J. B. Polley, "A Soldier's Letters to Charming Nellie.")

5. Eppa Hunton, *Autobiography*, 50.

6. Mary Boykin Chestnut, *A Diary from Dixie*, 95.

7. Robert E. Lee, *Lee's Dispatches*, unpublished letters of Lee to Jefferson Davis and the War Department of the C.S.A., 10. (Cited hereafter as Lee.)

8. Armistead L. Long, *Memoirs of Robert E. Lee*, 29.

9. *Heth Memoirs*, 152.

10. SHSP, XXVIII, 297.

11. Maury, 229.

12. Richmond *Examiner*, November 1861.

13. Robert Stiles, *Four Years Under Marse Robert*, 111.

14. Bell I. Wiley, "The Story of Three Southern Small Unit Commanders," *Civil War Times Illustrated* (April 1964), 9.

15. Val C. Giles, *Rags and Hope*, 49.

16. *Battles and Leaders of the Civil War*, II, 538. (Cited hereafter as B&L.)

17. Percy Gatling Hamlin, *Old Bald Head*, 73. (Cited hereafter as Hamlin's Ewell.)

18. Longstreet, 59.

19. Hood, 30.

20. Susan Leigh Blackford, compiler, *Letters from Lee's Army*, 38–39.

21. Ibid., 110–11.

22. *Heart of a Soldier*, 48–49.

23. Ibid., 66.

24. Ben Perley Poore, *Life and Public Service of Ambrose E. Burnside*, 39–40.

25. James C. Birdsong, *Brief Sketches of North Carolina Troops in the War Between the States*, 54.

26. B&L, III, 101.

27. Sorrel, 92.

28. Fleming, 187.

29. Theodore Lyman, *Meade's Headquarters—1863–1865*, 110–11.

30. Ibid., 111.

31. William W. Hassler, *A. P. Hill, Lee's Forgotten General*, 22.

(Citing George B. McClellan mss., a letter from Mary T. Jackson to Mrs. McClellan, Nov. 3, 1863.)
32. Henry Kyd Douglas, *I Rode with Stonewall*, 178.

Chapter 3:
The Leaders

1. An English Combatant, *Battlefields of the South*, 333.
2. Sorrel, 26.
3. E. M. Coulter, *Lost Generation*, 78.
4. SHSP, V, 192.
5. G. F. R. Henderson, *Stonewall Jackson*, 318.
6. Ibid., 319.
7. Pender, 171.
8. Papers of Zebulon B. Vance, 443.
9. George M. Neese, *Three Years in the Confederate Horse Artillery*, 19.
10. Chestnut, 330.
11. Stiles, 223.
12. Sorrel, 128.
13. Ibid., 48.
14. J. B. Polley, *Hood's Texas Brigade*, 54.
15. Alice Maude Ewell, *A Virginia Scene or Life in Old Prince William County*, 64.
16. Richard Taylor, *Destruction and Reconstruction*, 37.
17. Ibid.
18. Hamlin's Ewell, 138.
19. O.R., XII, Part 3, 890.
20. O.R., XIX, Part 2, 643.
21. Jedediah Hotchkiss, *Make Me a Map of the Valley*, 87.
22. Washington *Post* interview, July 11, 1893.
23. Hal Bridges, *Lee's Maverick General*, 6.
24. William Couper, *One Hundred Years at V.M.I.*, I, 189.
25. Bridges, 37.
26. William C. Oates, *War Between the Union and the Confederacy*, 398.
27. Bridges, 33.
28. Chestnut, 300.

Chapter 4:
"A Contempt for Danger"

1. Bridges, 47.
2. John C. Haskell, *The Haskell Memoirs*, 32.
3. Pender, 171.
4. W. A. Montgomery, *Life and Character of Maj. Gen. W. D. Pender*, 7.
5. James Arthur Lyon Fremantle, *The Fremantle Diary*, 127.
6. James Cooper Nisbet, *Four Years on the Firing Line*, 123.
7. Chestnut, 395.
8. Douglas Southall Freeman, *Lee's Lieutenants*, II, 620n, quoting Lee letter to Wilcox, Nov. 12, 1863.
9. Ibid., II, 701n, quoting Wilcox letter to his sister, May 16, 1863.
10. William Dorsey Pender Papers.
11. O.R., XXV, Part 2, 810.
12. Stephen Dodson Ramseur Papers.
13. William Dorsey Pender Papers.
14. Pender, 191.
15. Lafayette McLaws Papers.
16. SHSP, XX, 384.
17. *Histories of the Several Regiments and Battalions from North Carolina in the Great War, 1861–1865*, IV, 164–65. (Cited hereafter as N.C. Regts.)
18. Douglas, 38.
19. Pender, 229.
20. B&L, III, 245.
21. *The Record*, I (1863), 41–42. (Periodical published in Richmond.)

Chapter 5:
"A Handful of Lieutenants"

1. Fleming, 180.
2. Dennis H. Mahan, *Advanced Guard, Outpost and Detachment Service of Troops with the Essential Principles of Strategy*, 165.
3. Ibid., 200.
4. Ibid., 165.

5. Ibid., 216.
6. Fremantle, 187–88.
7. O.R., XIX, Part 2, 718.
8. Lee, 284.
9. Fremantle, 191.
10. Haskell, 55–56.
11. Fleming, 172–73.
12. J. F. C. Fuller, *War and Western Civilization,* 99.
13. Sir Garnet Wolseley, *General Sherman,* 99–101.
14. Hood, 53.

Chapter 6:
"A Desperate Thing to Attempt"

1. SHSP, IV, 152.
2. Pender, 242.
3. B&L, III, 285.
4. John B. Gordon, *Reminiscences of the Civil War,* 157.
5. Pender, 253.
6. SHSP, XXXIV, 327.
7. Clifford Dowdey, *Death of a Nation,* 270.
8. June Kimble, *Confederate Veteran* (Oct. 1910), 460.
9. Randolph A. Shotwell, *Our Living and Dead,* IV, 90.
10. George R. Stewart, *Pickett's Charge,* 144.
11. Fitzhugh Lee, *General Lee,* 64. (Lee to Mrs. Lee, Nov. 5, 1855.)
12. SHSP, XXXI, 228–36.
13. Francis W. Dawson, *Reminiscences of Confederate Service,* 96.
14. SHSP, XXXII, 189.
15. B&L, III, 373.
16. SHSP, IV, 107.
17. Alexander, 423.
18. SHSP, XXXII, 186.
19. Mrs. LaSalle Corbell Pickett, *Pickett and His Men,* 302.
20. B&L, III, 387.
21. SHSP, XXXVIII, 317.
22. Dawson, 97.
23. SHSP, XXXII, 37.
24. Fremantle, 212.
25. Ibid., 215.

26. SHSP, X, 428.

27. J. T. James, *Confederate Veteran*, (Sept. 1894).

28. Taylor, 89.

29. *Letters of Gen. James C. Connor*, edited by Mary C. Moffett, 115.

30. Randolph McKim, *A Soldier's Recollections*, 134.

31. Lee, 92.

32. Jacob Hoke, *The Great Invasion*, 161.

33. Long, 311.

34. *Confederate Military History*, III, 460.

35. *The Civil War Diary of Gen. Josiah Gorgas*, 111.

Chapter 7:
"Who Could You Put in His Place?"

1. Stiles, 223–24.

2. Lafayette McLaws Papers.

3. Walter H. Taylor mss.

4. Hood, 55.

5. Gorgas, 100.

6. Stiles, 247.

7. *Heth Memoirs*, 27.

8. Ibid., 31.

9. W. J. Robertson, *"Up Came Hill"—Soldier of the South*, Richmond *Times-Dispatch*, (Oct. 21, 1934).

10. *Heth Memoirs*, 184.

11. Ibid., 185.

12. Gen. Horace Porter, *Campaigning with Grant*, 110–11.

13. Gordon, 284–85.

14. Lyman, 152.

15. SHSP, XXXII, 208.

16. Lee, 255–56.

17. Hamlin's Ewell, 130.

18. *Confederate Veteran*, XIX, 531.

19. H. B. McClellan, *I Rode with Jeb Stuart*, 415.

20. Ibid., 416.

21. SHSP, XXXVII, 68.

22. Douglas Southall Freeman, *R. E. Lee*, III, 331.

Chapter 8:
"My Bad Old Man"

1. Jennings Wise, *The End of an Era*, 228.
2. Ibid., 228.
3. Douglas, 33.
4. Sorrel, 50.
5. Stiles, 189.
6. Jubal A. Early, *Autobiographical Sketch and Narrative of the War Between the States*, xvi–xvii.
7. Ibid., xviii.
8. O.R., XLIII, Part 1, 609–10.
9. Frank E. Vandiver, *Jubal's Raid*, 39.
10. Early, 392.
11. Susan Pendleton Lee, *Memoirs of William Nelson Pendleton, D.D.*, 363.
12. Henry Robinson Berkeley diary, entry of July 24, 1864.
13. Douglas, 311.
14. Ibid., 314.
15. Stephen Dodson Ramseur Papers.
16. Ibid.
17. Douglas, 317.
18. Schaff, 56–57.
19. O.R., XLIII, Part 1, 562–63.
20. "Memoirs of Major Edward H. McDonald of Winchester, Va.," *Civil War Times Illustrated* (February 1968), 44.
21. Freeman's *R. E. Lee*, IV, 507–09.
22. Douglas, 324.

Chapter 9:
"The Gallant Hood of Texas"

1. Old Records Division, Adjutant General's Office, Washington, D.C.
2. Chestnut, 297.
3. Polley, 142.
4. Ibid., 143.
5. William Dorsey Pender Papers.

6. Giles, 151.
7. Sorrel, 127.
8. Chestnut, 379.
9. Thomas Cooper DeLeon, *Four Years in Rebel Capitals*, 178–79.
10. Chestnut, 381.
11. Mrs. D. Giraud Wright, *A Southern Girl in '61*, 114.
12. Sorrel, 127–28.
13. O.R., XXIX, Part 2, 743.
14. Richard O'Connor, *Hood: Cavalier General*, 252.
15. Chestnut, 326.
16. Ibid., 368.
17. O.R., XXXVIII, Part 5, 881 and XXXIX, Part 2, 712–13.
18. Lee, 284.
19. Sam R. Watkins, *Co. Aytch*, 178.
20. Richmond *Whig*, July 20, 1864.
21. W. T. Sherman, *Personal Memoirs*, II, 72.
22. New York *Times*, Oct. 31, 1864.
23. O.R., xxxviii, Part 5, 888.
24. Watkins, 238.
25. Ibid., 241.
26. Ibid.
27. Maury, 149.
28. Chestnut, 474.

Chapter 10:
"The Marks of Hard Service"

1. J. William Jones, *Personal Reminiscences, Anecdotes and Letters of Gen. R. E. Lee*, 40.
2. Chestnut, 428.
3. Gordon, 416.
4. Douglas, 328.
5. Stiles, 311.
6. Douglas, 322.
7. Gordon, 417.
8. SHSP, V, 176.
9. Wise, 331.
10. Rush L. Hawkins, *An Account of the Assassination of Loyal Citizens of North Carolina*, 25. (Cited hereafter as Hawkins.)

11. Capt. John G. Smith, *Carolina and the Southern Cross*, (April 1914, Vol. 2, No. 1).
12. Ibid.
13. Hawkins, 27–28. (Pickett letter to Maj. Gen. John J. Peck, Feb. 17, 1864).
14. Ibid., 36. (Endorsement by Edwin M. Stanton, June 19, 1865).
15. O.R., XXVII, Part 3, 1075.
16. Wise, 338.
17. Longstreet, 583–87.
18. Charles S. Dwight, *A South Carolina Rebel's Recollections*, 5.
19. Sorrel, 256.
20. Gordon, 382.
21. LaSalle Corbell Pickett, 386.
22. Philadelphia *Weekly Times*, April 5, 1885.
23. "Proceedings of the Court of Inquiry in the case of Gouverneur K. Warren," Washington, D.C., 481.
24. Long, 410.
25. SHSP, XIX, 185.
26. SHSP, XI, 568.
27. Freeman's *Lee's Lieutenants*, III, 679. (W. H. Palmer to W. H. Taylor, June 25, 1905.)
28. Douglas, 330.
29. B&L, IV, 725.
30. Richard O'Connor, *Sheridan the Inevitable*, 265.
31. Frederic C. Newhall, *With General Sheridan in Lee's Last Campaign*, 188.
32. William Mahone, "On the Road to Appomattox," *Civil War Times Illustrated* (January 1971), 10.
33. Freeman's *R. E. Lee*, IV, 112.
34. Longstreet, 620.
35. Brig. Gen. John Gibbon, *Personal Recollections of the Civil War*, 318.
36. Ibid., 320.
37. *Heth Memoirs*, 199.
38. Henry E. Tremain, *Last Hours of Sheridan's Cavalry*, 266.
39. New Orleans *Times-Democrat*, May 8, 1892.

Chapter 11:
"Those of Us Who Are Left Behind"

1. Columbia *Daily Record*, June 29, 1879.
2. Burnside, 270–71.
3. Dictionary of American Biography, Vol. VI, 357.
4. *History of the Mexican War* was edited by his niece, Mary Rachel Wilcox, and published in 1892 after his death.
5. Jonathan Truman Dorris, *Pardon and Amnesty Under Lincoln and Johnson*, 166.
6. Hamlin's Ewell, 198.
7. Wright, 230–31.
8. Haskell, 134n.
9. Haskell, 18.
10. Hawkins, 37–38. (Pickett letter to Grant, March 12, 1866.)
11. Ibid., 39. (Grant to Johnson, March 16, 1866.)
12. John S. Mosby, *Memoirs*, 380–81.
13. Donald Bridgman Sanger and Thomas Robson Hay, *James Longstreet*, 415.
14. Washington *Post* interview, June 11, 1893.
15. SHSP, XXIII, 238–47.
16. Eppa Hunton, *Autobiography*, 98.
17. W. W. Blackford, *War Years with Jeb Stuart*, 229.
18. Ibid., 49–50.
19. Haskell, 55–56.
20. William Mahone, "On the Road to Appomattox," *Civil War Times Illustrated* (January 1971), 47.
21. Lafayette McLaws Papers.
22. SHSP, XI, 187.

Bibliography

Sources for *Rebels from West Point* have been grouped in four categories: General Works, Periodicals and Collections, Manuscripts and Letters, and Newspapers.

General Works

Alexander, E. Porter. *Memoirs of a Confederate.* New York, 1907.

Austin, Aurelia. *Georgia Boys with Stonewall Jackson.* Athens, 1967.

Birdsong, James C. *Brief Sketches of North Carolina Troops in the War Between the States.* Raleigh, 1894.

Blackford, Susan Leigh, compiler. *Letters from Lee's Army.* New York, 1947.

Blackford, W. W. *War Years with Jeb Stuart.* New York, 1945.

Bridges, Hal. *Lee's Maverick General.* New York–Toronto–London, 1961.

Casler, John O. *Four Years in the Stonewall Brigade.* Guthrie, Okla., 1893.

Chestnut, Mary Boykin. *A Diary from Dixie.* New York, 1905.

Commager, Henry Steele. *The Blue and the Gray.* Indianapolis–New York, 1950.

Connor, James C. *Letters of Gen. James C. Connor.* Edited by Mary C. Moffett. Columbia, S.C., 1933.

Coulter, E. M. *Lost Generation.* Tuscaloosa, Ala., 1956.

Couper, William. *One Hundred Years at the Virginia Military Institute.* Richmond, 1939.

Cullum, G. W. *Biographical Register of the Officers and Graduates of the U.S. Military Academy from 1802 to 1867.* Boston, 1891.

Dawson, Francis W. *Reminiscences of Confederate Service.* Charleston, 1882.

DeLeon, Thomas Cooper. *Four Years in Rebel Capitals.* New York, 1962.

Dorris, Jonathan Truman. *Pardon and Amnesty Under Lincoln and Johnson.* Chapel Hill, 1953.

Douglas, Henry Kyd. *I Rode with Stonewall.* Chapel Hill, 1940.

Dowdey, Clifford. *Death of a Nation.* New York, 1958.

Dwight, Charles S. *A South Carolina Rebel's Recollections.* Columbia, S.C., 1917.

√Early, Jubal Anderson. *Autobiographical Sketch and Narrative of the War Between the States.* Philadelphia, 1912.

Eggleston, George C. *A Rebel's Recollections.* New York, 1875.

Eliot, Ellsworth, Jr. *West Point in the Confederacy.* New York, 1941.

English Combatant, Anon. *Battlefields of the South from Bull Run to Fredericksburg.* New York, 1864.

Ewell, Alice Maude. *A Virginia Scene or Life in Old Prince William County.* Lynchburg, 1901.

Fleming, Thomas J. *West Point—The Men and Times of the U.S.M.A.* New York, 1969.

Forman, Sidney. *A History of the U.S. Military Academy.* New York, 1950.

Freeman, Douglas Southall. *R. E. Lee. A Biography.* 4 Vols. New York–London, 1935.

———. *Lee's Lieutenants.* 3 Vols. New York, 1945.

Fremantle, James Arthur Lyon. *The Fremantle Diary.* Editing and commentary by Walter Lord. Boston, 1954.

Fuller, J. F. C. *War and Western Civilization, 1832–1932.* London, 1932.

Gibbon, John. *Personal Recollections of the Civil War.* New York, 1928.

Giles, Val C. *Rags and Hope.* Memoirs compiled and edited by Mary Laswell. New York, 1961.

Gordon, John B. *Reminiscences of the Civil War.* New York, 1903.

Gorgas, Josiah. *The Civil War Diary of Gen. Josiah Gorgas.* Edited by Frank E. Vandiver. University, Ala., 1947.

Hamlin, Percy Gatling. *Old Bald Head.* Strasburg, Va., 1940.

Hancock, A. R. *Reminiscences of Winfield Scott Hancock.* New York, 1887.

Haskell, John C. *The Haskell Memoirs.* Edited by Gilbert E. Govan and James W. Livingood. New York, 1960.

Hassler, William W. *A. P. Hill: Lee's Forgotten General.* Richmond, 1957.

Hawkins, Rush C. *An Account of the Assassination of Loyal Citizens of North Carolina.* New York, 1897.

Henderson, G. F. R. *Stonewall Jackson.* London–New York, 1898.

Hoke, Jacob. *The Great Invasion.* New York–London, 1959.

Hood, John Bell. *Advance and Retreat.* New Orleans, 1880.

Hotchkiss, Jedediah. *Make Me a Map of the Valley.* Dallas, 1973.

Hunton, Eppa. *Autobiography.* Richmond, 1933.

Jones, J. William. *Personal Reminiscences, Anecdotes and Letters of Gen. Robert E. Lee.* New York, 1874.

Lee, Fitzhugh. *General Lee.* Greenwich, Ct., 1961.

Lee, Robert E. *Lee's Dispatches.* Unpublished letters of General Robert E. Lee, C.S.A., to Jefferson Davis and the War Department of the Confederate States of America, 1862–65. Edited with an introduction and notes by Douglas Southall Freeman. New York, 1957.

✓Lee, Susan Pendleton. *Memoirs of William Nelson Pendleton, D.D.* Philadelphia, 1893.

Long, Armistead L. *Memoirs of Robert E. Lee.* London, 1886.

✓Longstreet, James. *From Manassas to Appomattox.* Philadelphia, 1896.

Lyman, Theodore. *Meade's Headquarters, 1863–65.* Boston, 1922.

McClellan, H. B. *I Rode with Jeb Stuart.* Bloomington, Ind., 1958.

McKim, Randolph H. *A Soldier's Recollections.* New York, 1910.

Mahan, Dennis Hart. *Advanced Guard, Outpost and Detachment Service of Troops with the Essential Principles of Strategy.* New York, 1864.

Maury, Dabney H. *Recollections of a Virginian in the Mexican, Indian and Civil Wars.* New York, 1894.

Moore, Edward A. *The Story of a Cannoneer Under Stonewall Jackson.* New York, 1907.

✓ Morrison, James L., Jr. *The Memoirs of Henry Heth.* Westport, Ct., 1974.

✓Mosby, John S. *Memoirs.* Edited by Charles W. Russell. Boston, 1917.

Neese, George M. *Three Years in the Confederate Horse Artillery.* Washington, 1911.

Newhall, Frederic C. *With General Sheridan in Lee's Last Campaign.* Philadelphia, 1866.

Nisbet, James C. *Four Years on the Firing Line.* Jackson, Tenn., 1963.

Oates, William C. *War Between the Union and the Confederacy.* New York, 1905.

O'Connor, Richard. *Hood: Cavalier General.* New York, 1949.

———. *Sheridan, the Inevitable.* Indianapolis, New York, 1953.

Owen, William M. *In Camp and Battle with the Washington Artillery of New Orleans.* Boston, 1885.

✓Pender, William Dorsey. *The General to His Lady—The Civil War Letters of William Dorsey Pender to Fanny Pender.* Edited by William W. Hassler. Chapel Hill, 1962.

✓Pickett, George E. *Heart of a Soldier. Pickett's War Letters to His Wife.* Compiled and edited by LaSalle Corbell Pickett. New York, 1913.

————. *Soldier of the South. Pickett's War Letters to His Wife.* An expanded edition edited by Arthur Crew Inman. Boston, 1928.

✓Pickett, LaSalle Corbell. *Pickett and His Men.* Atlanta, 1899.

Polley, J. B. *Hood's Texas Brigade, Its Marches, Its Battles, Its Achievements.* New York, 1910.

Poore, Ben Perley. *Life and Public Service of Ambrose E. Burnside.* Providence, 1882.

✓Porter, Horace. *Campaigning with Grant.* Bloomington, Ind., 1961.

Ratchford, James W. *Some Reminiscences of Persons and Incidents of the Civil War.* Austin, Tex., 1971.

Sanger, Donald Bridgman, and Thomas Robson Hay. *James Longstreet.* Baton Rouge, 1952.

Schaff, Morris. *The Spirit of Old West Point.* New York, 1907.

✓ Sheridan, Philip H. *Personal Memoirs.* New York, 1888.

✓Sherman, William Tecumseh. *Personal Memoirs.* New York, 1875.

Shotwell, Randolph A. *The Papers of . . . ,* edited by J. G. de R. Hamilton. Raleigh, 1929.

✓ Sorrel, G. Moxley. *Recollections of a Confederate Staff Officer.* New York, 1917.

Stewart, George R. *Pickett's Charge.* Boston, 1959.

Stiles, Robert. *Four Years Under Marse Robert.* Washington, 1903.

Taylor, Richard. *Destruction and Reconstruction.* New York, 1879.

Tremain, Henry E. *Last Hours of Sheridan's Cavalry.* New York, 1904.

Vance, Zebulon B. *Papers of . . . ,* edited by Frontis W. Johnston. Raleigh, 1963.

Vandiver, Frank E. *Jubal's Raid.* New York, 1960.

Watkins, Sam R. *Co. Aytch.* New York, 1962.

Welch, Spencer G. *A Confederate Surgeon's Letters to His Wife.* New York–Washington, 1911.

Wise, John S. *The End of an Era.* Boston, 1899.

Worsham, John H. *One of Jackson's Foot Cavalry.* New York, 1912.

Wright, Mrs. D. Giraud. *A Southern Girl in '61.* New York, 1905.

Periodicals and Collections

Battles and Leaders of the Civil War, 4 vols., edited by Robert U. Johnson and Clarence C. Buel. New York, 1887–88.

Civil War Times Illustrated, Harrisburg, 1961— .

Confederate Military History, 12 vols., edited by Clement A. Evans. Atlanta, 1899.

Confederate Veteran, 40 vols. Nashville, 1893–1932.

Dictionary of American Biography, 20 vols. New York, 1928–37.

Our Living and Our Dead. Raleigh, 1874–76.

Southern Historical Society Papers, 49 vols. Richmond, 1876–1930.

U.S. War Department, *The War of the Rebellion, Official Records of the Union and Confederate Armies,* 128 vols. Washington, 1880–1901.

Manuscripts and Letters

Henry Robinson Berkeley Diary. Virginia Historical Society, Richmond.

Lafayette McLaws Papers. University of North Carolina, Chapel Hill.

William Dorsey Pender Papers. University of North Carolina, Chapel Hill.

Stephen Dodson Ramseur Papers. University of North Carolina, Chapel Hill.

Walter H. Taylor mss., in possession of Miss Janet F. Taylor, Norfolk, Va.

Newspapers

Columbia, S.C., *Daily Record*

New Orleans *Times-Democrat*

New York *Times*

Philadelphia *Weekly Times*

Richmond *Examiner*

Richmond *Times-Dispatch*

Richmond *Whig*

Washington *Post*

Index